WOMEN WITHIN RELIGIONS

WOMEN WITHIN RELIGIONS

Patriarchy, Feminism, and the Role of Women
in Selected World Religions

LOREEN MASENO
and
ELIA SHABANI MLIGO

Foreword by
ESTHER MOMBO

WIPF & STOCK · Eugene, Oregon

WOMEN WITHIN RELIGIONS
Patriarchy, Feminism, and the Role of Women in Selected World Religions

Wipf & Stock
An Imprint of Wipf and Stock Publishers
199 W. 8th Ave., Suite 3
Eugene, OR 97401

www.wipfandstock.com

PAPERBACK ISBN: 978-1-5326-9757-9
HARDCOVER ISBN: 978-1-4982-8732-6
EBOOK ISBN: 978-1-7252-4908-0

Manufactured in the U.S.A.   11/18/19

To Isaiah Ouma and Baraka Isaiah,
lifelong family and companions in life

To Ester J. Malekano, Upendo E. Mligo, Grace E. Mligo
and Faraja E. Mligo,
lifelong family and companions in life

CONTENTS

Chapter 9
ECOFEMINISM AND THE SACRED | 113

FOREWORD

THE ISSUES THAT SURROUND the role and place of women in religion have been discussed in the academy for many years now. While there are similarities in most religions about the role women play in different religions, there are also differences. What seems to be common in most religions is the position of women in a patriarchal society and how their role is determined in that system. Patriarchy which has been described by scholars of both religion and other studies as the rule of the father largely referring to a system of legal, social, economic, and political relations has existed for centuries. In relation to women, patriarchy is expressed in varied ways, including androcentricism and exclusion. Androcentrism is a male-centered worldview which values the male as the norm and devalues and or excludes and silences female perceptions, critiques, or contributions. The authors of this book deal with the history and development of patriarchy as shown by earlier scholars and how this has been challenged by readers of religion.

With this background, the book as a textbook sets out to introduce students to the basic tenets of patriarchy and how it has impacted on the roles that women have played in religion. The religions that have been used in this text include Islam, Hinduism, Buddhism, and African Traditional Religion, which are found in Africa in varied forms. The religious traditions are not dealt with in detail, as this is an introductory book which is meant to give as much for the student to interpret the context in which women work in each religious tradition; however, it creates enough interest for those who wish to carry more research to delve into each religious tradition in depth.

This book, written in an African context, touches difficult subjects such as feminism, which is an emotive word in the study of religion and or theology. The authors deal with the topic of feminism historically and the different theories within the movement. Feminism as a movement started in Europe and America in the nineteenth century. Aimed at bringing about the equal and full liberation of women in all aspects of life, feminism was based on the belief that much of the history of humankind has been patriarchal, and in order for change to occur, there needed to be a major force or revolution. The authors of this book delve into the different schools of thought and theories of feminism. In a simple analysis, the authors look at the different stages of feminism, showing the key players in the movement, especially in academia. The three waves of feminism are discussed with their major achievements, making the narrative easy to grasp. Feminism has been appropriated by different women in bringing to light their experiences as per their context. While it began in the Euro-American context, it has been renamed and redefined in its context of origin and in other contexts as well. For instance, the women of color in America in the 1980s began to define their form of feminism as "womanist," arguing that one could not separate the racial issues from the discussions on gender. The women from Latin America known as *mujerista* women brought into the study of feminism marginalization in the context of North America. Women from other parts of the world like Asia brought to the fore issues of religious, cultural and racial pluralism. The issues confronting women in Asia include rape, dowry deaths, and women enslavement in their homes. For African feminist theologians, they bring to the table the legacies of the colonial era and the problems facing the continent, including poverty, AIDs conflict, and war. With what is brought to the table of women's experiences, feminism is moved from academic circles to social movements that struggle for justice for women.

With this background, the authors of the book now delve into the different religious tradition and how they have impacted on women, especially the use of religious texts. Religious texts can be both oppressive and liberative depending on who is reading and interpreting the texts. The patriarchal and andocentric context has provided for men to read and interpret the texts which traditionally have pushed women to the margins. The texts are either oral and or written; both have been used to marginalize women. In view of dealing with the texts, as noted by women scholars, it is important that women read and interpret the texts to bring to light the liberative aspects rather than emphasizing the negative aspects of the texts. Of the religions that have been studied in this book, there are similarities in all, and three are good to highlight. First, the ideology of "patriarchy" governs the religious, social, political, and economic systems that ensure, preserve, and perpetuate male supremacy in all sectors of life. Second, the patriarchal ideology operates on the premise that men are biologically superior to women and that, as a result, women are weak and have to depend on men for survival. Third, male leadership, seen as the only legitimate leadership for the protection of women, is an overarching aspect of the book.

The women's reaction to Patriarchy is varied, but it can be described in two broad forms. On the one hand, women have internalized their own subordination and cooperated by accepting the sex-gender system. The women have then passed these values on to their children. Some of the reasons for women accepting the patriarchal position have been due to several things and or ways including indoctrination of the gender stereotypes, little or lack of education, division of women from each other, and defining women in accordance to their sexual abilities and through restraint and violence. The majority of women remain in this first form of subordination and cooperation. The other form of reaction is that where women have resisted cooption and presented a challenge to patriarchy.

This book deals with African women's theology, which is one form of reacting to patriarchy through academia in both research and writing. In this form of reaction, African women's theologies bring to light their experiences of God into the center of theological articulation.[1] As such, they reject the notion of maleness as the norm of humanity made in the image of God and instead see both female and male made in the image of God. In African women's theologies, sexism is named as sin and relationships are described as mutual. The thrust of African women's theologies include reclaiming what is positive in traditional culture and questioning that which is negative. For instance, in African traditional culture women participated in religious activities as priestesses, mediums, diviners, and medicine women, but within Christianity women are discriminated against, and manipulation of the supernatural rests largely in the hands of men. Casimir, Chukwuelobe, and Ugwu state more clearly about the role of Christianity and the church in Africa: "While women in Africa looked up to the colonial church as saviour that will liberate and restore their tradition-denied human rights and opportunities for human development, the Church supported the ancient and modern bearers of the culture to draw up and sustain a paternalist gender structure and constructs that perpetuated inequality and injustices against women."[2]

African women's theology as dealt with in this book brings to light women's voices in religion and culture that have been drowned by male theologies for almost three decades. With the publication of *Hearing and Knowing* in 1986, the missing voice of women began to emerge, even though from a distance. Oduyoye paved the way for African Christian women to tell their faith stories as they have heard and known them and not to rely on others to write about them. Out of this vision and commitment, Oduyoye

---

1. As Phiri asserts, the phrase "African women's theologies" is used in the plural, not in the singular. It is used in the plural "because African women theologians want to acknowledge the fact that even within Africa, there is diversity of women's experiences due to differences in race, culture, politics, economy and religions. Despite the differences in terminology, all women would like to see the end of sexism in their lives and the establishment of a more just society of men and women who seek the well-being of the other" (Phiri, "HIV/AIDS," 423).

2. Casimir et al., "Church and Gender Equality," 167.

began to look for her African women in churches and universities, who had undertaken or were undertaking theological and religious studies, to initiate a program of serious study, research, and publishing in religion and culture. Out of her efforts, and with the support of those who shared her passion, the idea of gathering a small group of African women theologians to launch an institute in religion and culture was conceived.

In 1989, the Circle of Concerned African Women Theologians (CCAWT), an interfaith institute, was launched in Ghana. During her opening address, Oduyoye urged women to do a "two-winged" theology, through which both women and men could communicate with God. The Circle has continued to meet after every six years under a theme which is researched and written about so that a publication is produced. It is through these publications that the Circle has attempted to demonstrate its vision, commitment, and lived experience in doing theology.

By taking the religious and cultural plurality in Africa seriously, the Circle embraces African women from all religions provided their concern and commitment is to participate in "doing" theology. The approach of doing theology from the Circle perspective is not in abstract ideas but dealing with issues that are life-threatening and/or destroying and life-giving and/or affirming. It is in this context that the Circle devoted over six years to the study of gender and HIV and AIDS, as well as the study of contemporary issues. The Circle has had work in other themes of theology, such as Christology and what it means to be church, as dealt with in this book.

While the study of African women's theology has been dealt with extensively in this book, one theme that cuts across all women's theologies is the study of ecofeminism. This topic is crucial as there is a correlation between the impoverishment of women and the impoverishment of the land. Deforestation impacts on women because it means they will walk twice for finding water and firewood. Pollution means that women will struggle more to obtain clean water for their families. It is in this context that Denise Ackermann and Tahira Joyner, writing in the context of South Africa, observed that "Earth-healing praxis requires an understanding of the interconnectedness of the different manifestations of violence. The violence of poverty, racism, sexism and classism, of social dislocation, of militarism, of battering and rape are not unrelated to the violence against the environment. They are all rooted in the abuse of power as domination over the exploitation of the other."[3] This book has indeed produced the basic understanding of all the above assertion in a coherent and clear development of thought.

Esther Mombo
Professor
St. Paul's University
Limuru, Kenya

---

3. Ackermann and Joyner, "Earth-Healing in South Africa," 125.

ACKNOWLEDGEMENTS

DIALOGUE WITH EACH OTHER and our students has enriched our lives in countless ways. We give thanks to God for this adventurous journey. We also appreciate the support of our colleagues at our current work stations (the department of religion, theology and philosophy at Maseno University in Kenya, and faculty of theology at Teofilo Kisanji University in Tanzania) for their invaluable comments on this project. We are indebted to copyeditors and typesetters of Wipf and Stock Publishers, especially Caleb Shupe and Ian Creeger respectively, for their excellent work. We also thank all those who in one way or another were involved in the completion of this book project.

We offer our thanks to all who are part of the faculty of theology at the University of Oslo, our colleagues and professors, especially Professor Jone Salomonsen, Professor Halvor Moxnes, Professor Kari Børresen, Professor Kjetil Hafstad, Professor Trygve Wyller, Professor Oddbjorn Liervik, and Professor Notto Thelle, whose challenges and expectations guided us to the successful completion of our PhD training. Their guidance and encouragement were invaluable during our training, and ultimately to the blossoming of this book project.

Furthermore, we are also deeply grateful for the support and encouragement we received from our spouses and children. Thank you very much for always believing in us, for many years of friendship, and for all the sacrifices made during the process of writing this book. This book is dedicated to you!

ABBREVIATIONS

AIDS	Acquired Immune Deficiency Syndrome
CCAWT	The Circle of Concerned African Women Theologians
BCE	Before Common Era
CE	Common Era
EATWOT	The Ecumenical Association of Third World Theologians
HIV	Human Immunodeficiency Virus
PhD	Philosophiae Doctor
USA	United States of America

INTRODUCTION

TEACHING THE COURSE ON "Women within Religions" at a university in a developing country over some years brings to the fore gaps in materials in regard to the course content. Getting a course book that pays attention to women in African religion and at the same time covers other world religions is no easy task. However, having found this gap, we were encouraged by friends at the faculty of theology in Oslo, Norway to consider coming up with a book that would address this diversity. Therefore, this book responds to this urgent need. The book is about women's roles and transformative alternatives in world religious traditions in an effort to identify sources of empowerment, mutuality, and justice for both women and men.

This course book identifies and brings to the fore some materials on women in world religions, with a point of departure being women in African religion. We believe that the attempt made in this book will be of help to teachers and tutors of "Women within Religions" course and related courses in tertiary institutions of learning. Furthermore, this book examines the position of women in religious traditions, beginning with an exploration of androcentric patterns of domination, and weaving through their grounding and legitimization in various religious traditions. We mainly feature women in Islam, Hinduism, Buddhism, and African religion. At the same time, the Christian textual tradition has a lot to offer on the place of women which we want students to engage in. In this case, this book will be a valuable tool to everyone interested in the place of women in world religions and traditions.

The synopsis of this book is simple. In chapters 1–3, we begin with the question of patriarchy and a brief survey of the theories underlying it. We move to the question of feminism, its history and the underlying theoretical perspectives, introduce the initiatives of African women towards the articulation of theology, their main themes of theologizing, the current debates in African women's theologies and their lived experiences. We also discuss the way African women theologians organize themselves to enhance unity in fighting their rights.

Chapter 4 launches the analysis of the place of women in world religions. We begin with the place of women in African Traditional Religion by discussing the way women were viewed before and after the dawn of Christianity and colonialism in the African soil. We also discuss the ideas of African women theologians on the issue of feminism and the place of women in African mythology and proverbs. Therefore, this chapter indicates the social origin and development of women consciousness that emanates from their interactions with various experiences of life from the time before and after Christianity and colonialism.

After the examination of the place of women in African Traditional Religion, chapter 5 introduces the place of women in Christian textual tradition. In this chapter we examine some Old and New Testament texts about women and the way they are depicted in those texts. Of great interest here are two women: Eve and Mary Magdalene. In chapters 6, 7, and 8 we examine the way women are depicted in Islam, Buddhism, and Hinduism respectively. We examine the various traditions in these religions and the way women have been considered and treated. The presentations of chapters are done in such a way that it is easy for someone to compare the place of women in one religion and another.

The book concludes with chapter 9 on ecofeminism and the sacred. Our foremost concern in this chapter is the link between issues raised in ecology and those raised in feminist movements. Two major levels of understanding the various concepts in this chapter have been suggested: the cultural symbolic and the social economic levels. In this case, having chapter review questions at the end of each chapter to enable readers to reconceptualize what they have read, the book will be useful not only to feminist theologians who strive to locate women at an equal footing with men in various aspects of human life, but also to all teachers and students of feminist religious studies in various institutions of higher learning.

FACES OF GENDER INEQUALITY

1) Harmful traditional practices (HTP) that affect women such as female genital mutilation (FGM) and harmful delivery practices (trial women to squat during delivery);

2) Food taboos (not allowed to eat certain foods or some choicest parts of meat such as gizzard);

3) Early girl child marriages;

4) Forced girl child prostitution for family economic survival;

5) Forced girl child labour;

6) Forced girl child soldiers/combatants in conflict;

7) Girl childhood scarification of the face;

8) Male child preference over the girl child;

9) Unequal Access to Education (girl child education suppressed/ Denied her);

10) Denial of property inheritance rights to the girl child/ daughter;

11) Wrongful widowhood practices—such as inhuman and degrading treatment of women who have lost their husbands;

12) Exclusion of women from governance and socio-economic policy planks;

13) Denial of reproductive health rights to women;

14) Sexual and other forms of (marital rape etc.) domestic influence;

15) Political marginalization of women in Africa (non-implenetation[sic] of affirmative gender rights in political appointments etc.);

16) Electoral violence against women;

17) Embedded Bias against women in the legal system and other professional associations;

18) Patriarchal dogma and biased interpretation of Africa cultural cosmology and ontology of gender equality.

19) Stoning women to death as a result of adultery of alleged.[4]

---

4. Madu in Casimir *et al.*, "Church and Gender Equality," 172.

Chapter 1

THE CONCEPT OF PATRIARCHY

INTRODUCTION

WE BEGIN THIS CHAPTER by stating the situation in the relationship between men and women in the United States in the nineteenth century before the emergence of the women's rights movement. We also state the common goal of human beings towards one another. Lochhead states the situation in the United States:

> The early nineteenth century in America was a time of rapid industrial growth with a growing middle class and increasing personal wealth. As men left the house to take jobs, women maintained the domestic sphere. They were responsible for raising children, encouraging religious study, and maintaining moral order at home. Society expected proper women to be submissive, pious, and engaged in domestic affairs. As Barbara Welter explained in her seminal article "Cult of True Womanhood: 1820–1860," people believed that a virtuous and pious woman could save a man's soul from destruction through her moral perfection and domesticity. A timid attitude, dependence on one's husband, piety, and a submissive disposition defined true femininity. If women chose not to be submissive, society interpreted their

behavior as an attack on the natural order of the universe and a threat to societal norms."[1]

The central question regarding this relationship is whether there was justice, equality, and mutual caring between men and women in the United States during this period. However, David Russel states the goal of human beings towards one another as they live in this world:

> We are all called by the very nature of our humanity to work for a shared human community characterised by justice, equity and mutual caring. It is these qualities and values that enable us as fellow human beings, to fulfil our true human potential together, cherishing creation. However, there are many forces pitted against this commitment to human flourishing, and their roots grow deep. They become manifest in attitudes, behaviours and structures that undermine our human endeavours.[2]

Russel further asserts that the main obstacle to implementing the above stated goal is the resurgence of patriarchy in world societies, which makes human relations asymetrical, as was in America's situation before the women's movement for equality. Patriarchy, according to him, distorts the relationship arrangements in our current societies and the way "relationships have been structured, assumed and imposed" throughout history.[3]

The question is, what is patriarchy and how does it work? Patriarchy, as a concept, is not easy to define because of having a combination of meanings. However, our starting point in defining patriarchy is this question: Is patriarchy a system, a category, or a concept? In this chapter, we attempt to help students understand what patriarchy is and, better still, operationalize it in various

---

1. Lochhead, "Turning the World Upside Down," 5.

2. Russel, "Introduction to the Publication," 2.

3. Russel, "Introduction to the Publication," 2. However, Maluleke calls patriarchal ideas that have influenced human relationships, especially between men and women throughout African theology, "supremacist ideology, i.e. it speaks to the supremacy of the male" (see Maluleke, "African Theology," 31; cf. Chisale, "Patriarchy and Resistance," 13–14).

religious contexts. The etymology of the term "patriarchy" is the Latin word *Patriarche*. This word is formed by two Greek words: *pater*, which means "father," and *arche*, which means "rule." Therefore, following this etymology, the word "patriarchy" means "rule of the father." In the popular discussions of the time it was more often used to refer to the "rule of men over women."

According to Wood, "Patriarchy is defined as the 'rule of the father' in a male-dominated family and as a social and ideological construct which considers men, as patriarchs, to be intrinsically superior to women."[4] Wood further notes that

> Patriarchy is a system in which women experience discrimination, subordination, violence, exploitation and oppression by men . . . In a patriarchal society, women are treated as inferior in all aspects of their lives; men control women's reproductive power, their sexuality, their mobility and even their economic resources.[5]

Hence, as Sultana puts it, "feminists use the term 'patriarchy' to describe the power relationship between men and women as well as to find out the root cause of women's subordination."[6]

Furthermore, Walby defines "patriarchy as a system of social structures and practices in which men dominate, oppress, and exploit women."[7] According to Walby, the use of the term "social structures" suggests that the domination, oppression, and exploitation which men exert over women is not biologically predetermined; and neither is that the man was created to rule and the woman created to be ruled by the man. In this case, patriarchy is a constructed social relation between men and women in a particular society.

Yet Epstein, quoting Becker, sees patriarchal social structures as being ubiquitous and existing in multiple forms. She states:

4. Wood, "Patriarchy, Feminism and Mary Daly," 14; cf. Maseno and Kilonzo, "Engendering Development," 45; Maseno-Ouma, "Patriarchy Ridiculed," 90–92; Selokela, "African Women," 3.

5. Wood, "Patriarchy, Feminism and Mary Daly," 14.

6. Sultana, "Patriarchy and Women's Subordination," 1.

7. Walby, *Theorizing Patriarchy*, 20.

"Patriarchal social structures have been tribal, monarchical, and totalitarian; dictatorial and democratic; nomadic, feudal, capitalist, and socialist; religious and atheistic; primitive and post-modern; tolerant and repressive of pornography."[8] Hence, its occurance in a particular situation and audience determines its meaning. To its broad sense, "patriarchy refers to the web of economic, political, social and religious regulations that enforced the domination of women by men throughout the ages."[9] Johannsdottir writes thus:

> We can go back beyond the birth of Christ to encounter patriarchy, when Aristotle and his often avante garde ideas blossomed. Aristotle assumed that women were the defective part of community, having only developed as a mistake when the temperature during conception was too low . . . During the Middle Ages this ideology was at its peak. Among renowned beliefs during this age was firstly that the woman was believed to be mainly driven by her libido and as a consequence she was blamed for the first sin ever committed in the sanctuary of Eden.[10]

Quoting in length from Johannsdottir in regard to the way the woman was considered and treated, Johannsdottir states:

> It is as if they were believed to be in some ways like children because of the social and psychological malfunctions, which early on brought their rank to a lower status than that of men. Their importance was primarily judged by looking at a few aspects of their lives, such as child rearing, how well they pledged themselves to their homes and how they did in civilizing their children and setting forth moral goals . . . The woman in earlier days was only considered to be one of the master's belongings just as any other property. Like an animal she was

---

8 Epstain, "Liberty, Patriarchy and Feminism," 90.

9 Maseno & Kilonzo, "Engendering Development," 45.

10 Johannsdottir, "Patriarchy and the Subordination of Women," 2; Sultana, "Patriarchy and Women's Subordination," 3–4.

supposed to show submission and obedience, which was the hallmark of a good wife.[11]

Therefore, the above quotation indicates that the woman was deprived of her esteem and society considered her as a play object. Maseno and Kilonzo firther insist that "Using a single word to describe the grand web of oppressive forces served the function of suggesting that male domination had a long history and stretched across national and cultural boundaries touching various facets of life. As such patriarchy invoked a sense of the enormity of the struggle ahead by identifying the enormity of the history that had bound women for centuries."[12] Therefore, based on the above allusions of the meaning of the word patriarchy, and the way the woman has been considered and treated in history, we can sum up that patriarchy is a word that connotes the unequal relationships between people of two sexes, male and female, which is a mere construction of society having nothing to do with divine predetermination.

Furthermore, the concept of patriarchy evokes an issue of the existence of a social system which is composed of coordinated relationships that have some sort of regularity. In this system, males are the ones who are considered having authority over women, exerting oppressive pressure in terms of social, political, and economic establishment. Therefore, due to its ability to capture the vast exploitative and oppressive structures existing between men and women, the concept of patriarchy remains a useful term in the field of feminism.[13]

According to radical feminist thinking, the concept of patriarchy plays a key role in analyzing the existing relations of systems and structures which are articulated in processes and institutions making them. Hartmann asserts that the definition of patriarchy can hardly be divorced from the cencept of system. As a system, it involves a set of social dealings having its basis in materials that

11. Johannsdottir, "Patriarchy and the Subordination of Women," 3.

12. Maseno and Kilonzo, "Engendering Development," 45.

13. Maseno and Kilonzo, "Engendering Development," 45.

operate on a system of male hierarchical relations and common-ness. To her, patriarchy is not universal and unchanging; rather, its intensity changes over time and place.[14]

For some feminists, patriarchy or the exclusion of women from history originates from the gender formation of males and females and the double standard entailed by this double standard. Ifechelobi puts it clearly: "A patriarchal society is a male dominated society. It is an institution of malerule and privilege that thrives on female subordination[;] that is why most forms of feminism characterize patriarchy as a wicked social system of rule that is oppressive to women because it is an exertion of male dominance over women."[15] Thus, structural changes in the marketplace and changes in wage structures allow patriarchy to begin occurring.

Mary Daly views patriarchy itself to be a religion of some sort; and this religion, according to her, exists in the whole life of human beings and is strongly held by all societies which carry on patriarchal ideas. In most cases, we agree with Okon, who states:

> Historically, religion has contributed to the marginaliza-tion of women. Religion has provided the platform for male domination of society. As a social anesthesia, and a lullaby that soothes and assuages revolutionary tenden-cies and hinders rebellion, religion has consoled women to accept their fate as the will of God. This is a negative social function and a distortion of reality, which led Karl Marx to describe religion as: "The sigh of the oppressed creature, the heart of a heartless world, just as it is the opium of the people."[16]

What Okon means here is that the resurgence of religious doc-trines has caused societies to take for granted the superiority of men over women and its consequence to their relationships.

Other scholars anchor themselves to women's reproduction. They attribute patriarchy to male control of women's reproduc-tion and fecundity in societies where patriarchy is being executed.

14. Humm, *Dictionary of Feminist Theory*, 200–202.

15. Ifechelobi, "Feminism," 18.

16. Okon, "Status of Woman," 21–22.

Moreover, some feminists consider patriarchy as analytically having no relationship with the capitalist mode of production or any other modes.[17] This notion means that "institutions and processes that compose patriarchal system are conceptualized as webs of gendered relations which sustain and reproduce male social power within various cultural sites, i.e., language, religion, media and popular culture, and education."[18] Hence, male social power in various cultures across Africa has contributed to the subjugation of women folk, resulting in countless occasions of male violence against women.

Male violence against women itself has a connotation. Male violence against women connotes a system of social control. Speaking more explicitly, male violence is a male weapon to exert control over women. Male violence, as a weapon of control, is manifested more in rape and domestic harassments. In this context, rape and domestic harassments are understood as being systemic and systematic activities mostly directed upon women and children. This has been seen and well-documented in conflict situations such as the Rwanda genocide, South Sudan, and even in the Democratic Republic of Congo.

Despite male violence as a weapon of control, there is a resurgence of political acts which maintain certain power relations in which most men are privileged regardless of whether or not they carry out acts of violence. In this situation, heterosexuality becomes a key institution of patriarchy used in organizing many aspects of gender relations. When heterosexuality is considered normal, all other forms of sexuality are considered abnormal because they do not propagate male hierarchy. Typically, patriarchal constructions of sexuality do the following: first, they reinforce heterosexuality; second, they assume men's sexuality as being assertive denying women's sexuality; and third, they expect women to remain virgins until marriage. Over and above these particular characterizations, each feminist theory finds that a different feature

17. Humm, *Dictionary of Feminist Theory*, 200–201.

18. Maseno and Kilonzo, "Engendering Development," 46; cf. Sultana, "Patriarchy and Women's Subordination."

of patriarchy defines women's subordination.[19] For example, on the one hand, radical feminists put patriarchy in an equal footing with male domination—they consider it as being a system concerned with social relations through which, between the two classes, one class—the class "men"—has power over the class "women" in consideration that women are devalued sexually.

The radical feminist emphasizes that, as a system, patriarchy oppresses women because of its paternal ascendance, organization, contestation, and powerfulness. For them, equality has the characteristics of divisions and dualisms which make it to be built upon the fundamentals of patriarchy. This either/or dichotomy is inherently and classically part of patriarchy. On the other hand, the socialist and Marxist feminists locate patriarchy in materialist context. They argue that the capitalist mode of production is structured by the sexual division of labor. Hence, the capitalist mode is criticized as being ahistorical because it argues that patriarchy can hardly be periodized like the Marxist modes of production.

Refraining from explicit deployment, most radical feminists are said to be descriptive in their use of patriarchy. Strictly speaking, patriarchy emphasizes the social construction of gender as a system of social hierarchy. In nature, this system is dynamic, and is not unchallengeable. Since patriarchy has had its varied history, and since it means different things to different theorists, in different times, recent theorists have made a combined effort to use it more precisely. They worry that if used as a broad umbrella to cover all forms of women's oppression, it would more possibly hide the multifaceted and constantly shifting character of injustices which women have suffered over the centuries.

There are differences within patriarchy. To imply that the Greco-Roman patriarchy and the patriarchy in present-day Africa are the same is not a valid conception. What is common is that there are historical contexts and, in each, dualisms are articulated that validate relations of domination and subordination. Consequently, this dualism orders societies hierarchically through a kinship style of patriarchal descent. However, the form and content

19. Maseno and Kilonzo, "Engendering Development."

of the relationships between the patriarchs (fathers) and women differ enormously.

Indeed, there is the idea that oppression results from a universal desire of men (the patriarchs) to dominate women and that men are biologically inclined to dominate women. This idea leads to the assumption that it is patriarchy which is the one to be blamed for women's oppression all over the world.[20] However, there are other structures and forces in society and culture, including the patriarchal kinship systems or the existing laws, which encourage the existence of patriarchy. Therefore, the concept of the "rule of the father" is not a monumental concept without other implications. It also implies that other males are ruled over apart from what is implied by "male domination."[21]

THEORIES OF PATRIARCHY

Having introduced the concept of patriarchy, we now turn to a brief look at some of the theories of this concept. Most theories of patriarchy have been criticized as purely descriptive and unable to explain the "origins" of male power. Some scholars who have tried to examine the origins of patriarchy have suggested theories related to the following issues:

1. Decline of matrilineal descent,

2. decline of goddess worship,

3. the development of agriculture, and

4. the development of warfare.

However, these theoretical perspectives can hardly claim to prove the origins of patriarchy because inquiries into origins always lack clear evidence. It is, therefore, better to see these theories as just contesting stories that try to put clear the possible problem of stories about origins of the unchallengeable place of patriarchy.

20. Jones, *Feminist Theory*, 77; cf. Russel, "Introduction to the Publication," 2.

21. Jones, *Feminist Theory*, 79–80.

Nevertheless, some of the ways which the theories of patriarchy have been using may exhibit a tendency to universalism, a phenomenon that hardly takes into account the profound differences amongst women, that is insensitive to historical location, cultural norms, and specificities.

CRITICISMS OF THE THEORIES OF PATRIARCHY

Having mentioned the theories of patriarchy in the above section, we now briefly state some of the criticisms posed upon them. We would like to state at the outset that the view of universal male domination is contested on various grounds. Serene Jones highlights some of these grounds as follows:

- It mistakenly suggests that all men are biologically predisposed to subjugate women. This kind of essentialism entraps men in a nature that appears inevitable. As such it becomes difficult to envision radical social change.

- When men become the sole focus, there is the tendency of having the conception of men as "enemy." There are incredibly few radical feminists who construe men as "enemies." This remains a simplistic reading of radical feminist theory that implies that all men oppress all women, and to the same extent and in the same ways. In so doing, we overlook the broad institution and cultural forces that harm women quite apart from the intentions of individual men.

- This monolithic view of patriarchy deflects attention from the effects of racism, heterosexism, ageism etc. on the lives of women. This makes the complexities of women's lives and the dimensions of women's experiences to be underestimated.[22]

Indeed, as highlighted by Jones above, some men have unequal power in patriarchal societies, especially when they are deemed to be "insufficiently masculine." Patriarchal theories have been accused of succumbing to a homogenizing conception of men as

22. Jones, *Feminist Theory*, 77–88.

being the "enemy." Yet, Walby contends that to deploy a theory of patriarchy does not mean to homogenize men, but it allows us to distinguish between "patriarchal men" from those who are not.[23] In this case, Walby's assertion warns us from generalizations that radical feminists have succumbed for a long time.

DEMYSTIFYING THE MYTH OF "UNIVERSAL MALE DOMINATION"

Having indicated that there is a concerted effort to use patriarchy more precisely, it is helpful for us now to consider some faces of oppression as elucidated by Serene Jones. Jones considers five faces of oppression:

- The first is oppression as exploitation. This face has to do with the specific dynamic point of view which relates to the distribution of labor and money. It assumes that often women are on the low-paying end of the production line, and that work at home is often not recalculated. Jones suggests that in order to understand oppression as exploitation, the Marxist and materialist feminist traditions do a material analysis of how material goods are produced and circulated in society and how jobs are distributed and money is made.

- The second is oppression as marginalization. Here, the focus on marginalization is the focus on people whom the system of labor cannot and will not use: for example, lesbians, gays, or the elderly, or even those infected and affected by HIV/AIDS.

- The third is oppression as powerlessness. This has to do with the way in which power is distributed and the way in which decisions are made. The important question here is who decides and for whose purpose?

- The fourth is oppression as cultural imperialism. This involves the way in which groups develop and apply cultural

23. Walby, *Theorizing Patriachy*, 19–24.

standards to define, interpret, and regulate beliefs; hence, attitudes and actions. Universalizing ones standards and imposing them on others.

- The fifth is oppression as violence. This face involves systematic and structural violence, which comprises of women's oppression. There are increasing numbers of assault, harassment, domestic violence, and sex-related violence. There is also fear of women and children being targets of physical and sexual abuse by men. References such as "slut," "bitch," and the like are means of controlling and opposing women's sexual autonomy while men's sexuality is celebrated. This double-standard life leads to the labeling of some women as being good and others as being bad. Hence, when we say it is systemic, we point out to the way in which various institutions and cultural beliefs and practices create a social climate where violence is not only imaginable but tolerated or accepted as "natural"—as being part of the human condition, e.g., during elections, circumcision ceremonies, etc. Jones notes that women are exploited in the home because of the division of work into the private and the public sections.[24]

Furthermore, Kandiyoti contends that women should strategize themselves within a set of concrete constraints that reveal and define what she calls the "patriarchal bargain." As a term, it is coined to denote a complex concept that indicates the existence of sets of rules and scripts regulating gender relations to which both genders accommodate and nonetheless may be contested, redefined, and renegotiated. The challenge with this term is the implicit meaning of "bargain," which denotes the existence of a deal between more or less equal participants.[25]

Nevertheless, the concept of "bargain," according to her, has different meanings depending on class, caste, and ethnicity. This means that patriarchal bargain is influential towards shaping women and their gendered subjectivity. Moreover, it determines

24. Jones, *Feminist Theory*, 78–80.
25. Kandiyoti, "Bargaining with Patriarchy," 286.

the nature of gender ideology held by people of various contexts. Similarly, patriarchal bargains influence both the potential for and specific forms of women's active or passive resistance in the face of their oppression. In sum, we can say that patriarchal bargains are not timeless or immutable entities; rather, they are subject to historical transformations which unfold new areas of struggles and dialogues between genders towards better relations.[26]

What then is the implication of the above assertion by Kandiyoti? Using examples, Kandiyoti shows the way women resisted attempts to lower the value of their labor, and more important, women refused to allow their husbands to appropriate them totally in terms of their production. However, problems developed when male household heads assumed that they would get the unremunerated labor of their wives. In Gambia, some men had to pay their wives wages or lend them an irrigated plot to have access to their labor. When labor was needed in all the farms, to show their autonomy, women were very strategic in their work. They chose to work first in their own plots and then afterwards on the plots of their respective husbands. In general, we can say that many women resisted projects that jeopardized the fragile balance in relationship with men which they strived to maintain. It appeared that non-corporations of the closely related family in ideology and practice informed marital and marketplace strategies for women.

Using examples from classic patriarchy exemplified in places such as North Africa, Turkey, Pakistan and Iran, India, and some parts of China, Kandiyoti maintains that in these places, girls are given away in marriage at a very young age into households headed by the father of the husband. The patriarchal lineage totally maintained a total appropriation of women rendering their work and contribution to production invisible. To Kandiyoti, the cyclical nature of women's power in the household and their anticipation of inheriting the authority of senior women encourage a thorough internalization of this form of patriarchy by the women themselves. Unlike women in sub-Saharan Africa who attempt to resist unfavorable labor relations in the household, women in areas

26. Kandiyoti, "Bargaining with Patriarchy," 275.

of classic patriarchy often adhere as far and as long as they possibly can to rules that result in the unfailing devaluation of their labor.[27] Yet, there are transformations involving materials. These material-based patriarchal transformations lead to crumbling new market forces, capital penetration in rural areas, etc. Thus, the breakdown of classical patriarchy results in the earlier emancipation of younger men from their fathers' control, and their wives then escape the control of mother-in-laws to head their own households at an early age. The generation of women caught in between it represents a personal tragedy as they had paid the heavy price of earlier patriarchal bargain but could not cash in on its promised benefits. Kandiyoti cites an example of increased suicides among women who are over forty-five, as opposed to the previous younger women, especially new brides, who killed themselves.[28]

Another example is about the Iranian women who adopt the veil. In so doing, the restriction of the Islamic order imposed on them makes their husbands have to work harder for security, stability, and presumed respect promised to them by this order. This is then a response by women in such places; it is their strategy.[29]

CONCLUSION

We conclude this chapter with Maseno and Kilonzo, that "There is a need to take into account the sum total of dominatory relations. Better still, systematic analyses of women's strategies and coping mechanisms . . . can help capture the nature of patriarchal systems in their cultural, class-specific, and temporal concreteness."[30] Systemic and systematic analysis of women's strategies also reveal the way in which men and women resist, accommodate, adapt, and conflict with each other over resources, rights, and responsibilities.

27. Kandiyoti, "Bargaining with Patriarchy," 178–280.
28. Kandiyoti, "Bargaining with Patriarchy," 282.
29. Kandiyoti, "Bargaining with Patriarchy," 283.
30. Maseno and Kilonzo, "Engendering Development," 47.

More practically, it is useful to focus on more narrowly defined patriarchal bargains than on an unqualified notion of patriarchy. Such a focus may be able to give better prospects for the detailed analysis of processes of transformation, as opposed to the unqualified notion of patriarchy.

CHAPTER REVIEW

1. In your own thinking, explain the meaning of the concept of patriarchy. How is patriarchy visible in your religion?

2. What is the relationship between power and patriarchy, and male domination and patriarchy, according to radical feminists?

3. Discuss the theories underlying patriarchy and male domination.

4. State the criticisms rendered to the practice of patriarchy?

5. How can the myth of universal male domination be demystified?

Chapter 2

FEMINISM, HISTORY, AND THEORY

INTRODUCTION

AFTER DISCUSSING THE CONCEPT of patriarchy we now turn to the issue of feminism. We analyze a brief history of feminism and its underlying theories. In fact, there are as many definitions of feminism in current scholarship as there are people who attempt to define this concept. This chapter will not attempt to provide a convincing definition of the concept of feminism, but will explore, albeit generally, the history of feminism as understood in recent times. This history will form the background to various feminist theories. Indeed, feminist theories did not develop in a vacuum; rather, they emerged alongside the social and cultural theories of their times. Therefore, as understood today, feminist theories encompass the thinking about not only gender, but also other demarcations of difference including race, sexuality, class, and other social categories.

BRIEF HISTORY OF FEMINISM

There are numerous understandings of feminism. Historically, Hebertine Auclert from France is considered to be the first person to use the word "feminism" in 1882 when naming the struggle of women to fight for their political rights.[1] In Africa, skeptics have not kept silent. They have rightly said that feminism hardly originates from Africa. The words of a novelist Buchi Emecheta captures this reality when she rejected the Western concept of feminism when she said:

> I will not be called feminist [. . .], because it is European. It is as simple as that. I just resent that . . . I don't like being defined by them . . . It is just that it comes from outside and I don't like people dictating to me. I do believe in the African type of feminism. They call it womanism, because, you see, you Europeans don't worry about water, you don't worry about schooling, you are so well off. Now, I buy land, and I say, "Okay, I can't build on it, I have no money, so I give it to some women to start planting." That is my brand of feminism.[2]

According to their view, feminism is a random mixture of complaints without order. They also view feminism to be a set of uncoordinated ideas with a power to change women's thinking and viewing of their exploitative and oppressive relationship with men in various spheres of life. They also insist, "Antisexism is not an issue in our world, where men and women know their place and play their role ungrudgingly and no one feels suffocated by the society's definition of femininity and masculinity. Issues of sexism are supposed to belong to a minority of disgruntled, leisure-saturated, middle class women of the capitalist west."[3]

Moreover, skeptics note that the concept of feminism embraces political and ideological connotations and view it as something

---

1. Clifford, *Introducing Feminist Theology*, 11, cf. Maseno and Kilonzo, "Engendering Development," 46.

2. Nfah-Abbenyi, *Gender in African Women's Writings*, 7.

3. Oduyoye, "Reflections," 249.

for a class of women merely struggling against male domination. Consequently, they add, "In Africa, feminism is often associated negatively with women who have 'difficulty' relating to men—that is, difficulty in keeping their marriages intact, through thick and thin. It is often said that women who talk of liberation are those whose ambitions in marriage have been frustrated."[4]

However, it should be recognized that the emphasis of African feminism is not so much to be in antagonistic relationship with men, but to have coexistence. This is a genuine African feminism, as reiterated by Steady, who is quoted by Ifechelobi thus: "A genuine African feminism recognizes a common struggle with African men for the removal of the yokes of foreign domination and European/American exploitation. It is not antagonistic to men but challenges them to be aware of certain salient aspects of women's subjugation which differ from the generalized oppression of all African peoples."[5]

It is an illusion to think that its influence is limited to the West and that it remains alien to Africa, though feminism originated from the West. There continues to be academic interaction and sharing between women from the West and Africa. A high number of African women have pursued their academic studies in the West, thus enhancing their interaction with ideas inherent in feminism. Indeed, Africa is not isolated or in a vacuum from varieties of ideas and thoughts owing to the movements of people and the help of technology. To insist that women and men in Africa know their place is to ignore gender oppressions inherent in the call to revert to traditional values. In so doing, this overlooks the gender construction of the public and private divide in African culture.

Though there are many definitions of feminism, the common idea in all definitions is human equality.[6] However, a useful definition is one articulated by Joann Wolski Conn, who says: "Feminism is both a set of coordinated ideas and a practical plan

4. Oduyoye, "Feminist Theology," 169.

5. Ifechelobi, "Feminism," 19.

6. Pillay, "Anglican Church," 61.

of action rooted in a critical awareness by women of how a culture controlled in meaning and action by men, for their own advantage oppresses women and dehumanizes men."[7] Moreover, Johansdottir defines feminism thus: "Feminism is the idea that women should have political, social, sexual, intellectual and economic rights equal to those of men. It involves various movements, theories and philosophies, all concerned with issues of gender difference, that advocate equality for women and the campaign for women's rights and interests."[8] Ifechelobi further states: "Feminism seeks to give the women a sense of self as worthy, effectual, and contributing human beings. It is a theoretical and ideological framework that directly opposes sexism by supporting gender equality. This is to say that feminism is a reaction to such stereotype of women, whereby women are seen as indeterminate human beings, dependent, gullible and voiceless. All these deny them a positive identity and fulfilment of self."[9] Within this understanding is the implication of praxis, thus resisting critics of feminist thought who say that feminism merely consists of uncoordinated ideas in a system of complaints. At the same time, it highlights that meaning in a culture can be controlled, for example by men.

FEMINIST THEORIES

It is clear that feminist theory from its inception has been pluralistic in nature. According to Rosemarie Tong, "feminist theory is not one but many theories or perspectives and each feminist theory or perspective attempts to describe women's oppression, to explain its causes and consequences and to prescribe strategies for women's liberation."[10] Each feminist theory finds that a different feature of patriarchy defines women's subordination.

---

7. Clifford, *Introducing Feminist Theology*, 17.

8. Jóhannsdóttir, "Patriarchy and the Subordination of Women," 6.

9. Ifechelobi, "Feminism," 20.

10. Tong and Botts, *Feminist Thought*, 1.

In the following paragraphs we will highlight Tong's ideas on the varieties of feminist thinking. According to Tong, liberal feminists insist on a form of women subordination based on a set of customary and legal constraints within which they must operate based on their sexual orientation. Liberal feminists contend that women's biological orientation is not a legitimate criterion to segregate women in social issues. Liberal feminism argues for equal representation of men and women in public arenas which men have dominion. The contribution of liberal feminism is its criticism of segregation of women in various social affairs based on sexual orientations. In so doing, it prompted the phenomenon of most women being incorporated in jobs that were previously male-dominated.

The radical feminist insists that patriarchy as a system oppresses women because it is characterized by paternal ascendance, power structure, competition, and powerfulness. Patriarchy has its root in the belief that women are different from and inferior to men, a belief that preoccupies the consciousness of men whenever they are in relationship with women. It is in the heart of radical feminists to assume that all males have a potential of exercising physical violence, such as rape and even murder, against females as their way of exercising power and control over them. Therefore, the concept of patriarchy becomes an important watch word for radical feminists.

The Marxist feminist comprehends female subordination as a result of the introduction of private property, therefore creating a class society. The modes of production available in a community and their control have an impact on who accesses privileges and power. To Marxist feminism, the unpaid housework which women perform creates classes of a male boss and a female worker. Moreover, the female economic dependence on their husbands is another source of their oppression.

A psychoanalytic feminist finds the root of women's oppression as being embedded deep in her psyche, as a result of group action and the internalization of non-interchangeable power structures in society and in homes. [11] According to this perspective, the submission of women to men happens due to their unconscious desire for emotional connectedness with men. When boys are born, they intimately adhere to and grow with the male mentalities of their fathers. Likewise, girls intimately adhere to and grow in the female emotion and mentalities of their mothers. Thus femininity and masculinity become identities that differentiate between people of the two sexes.

The socialist feminist endeavors to weave the strands of feminist theory together. The goal is to relate the myriad of forms of women's oppression. Generally, the socialist feminist understands that there are only complex explanations for female subordination. To the existentialist feminist, woman is oppressed by virtue of "otherness," implying that woman is regarded as the "other" because she is not-man. Unlike other feminist thoughts that attempt to find integration and agreement to represent how women see the world, the postmodernist feminist refuses to center and cement separate thoughts by overemphasizing difference. [12] Therefore, the socialist, Marxist, and psychoanalytic feminisms criticize the use of a family and the interaction that exists there as a source of exploiting or suppressing women.

Tong spells out perspectives from which to interrogate feminist theories. In sum, she selects what in her view are legitimate approaches by feminists. However, her selection does not take into account, among others, post-colonial approaches or even black feminist perspectives. These are a challenge to white-dominated feminism and a call for a more broad-based understanding that allows for different cultural/racial communities and politics. In this postcolonial space, it is clear that women experience multiple dilemmas of tradition and modernity which conflict and contrast with each other. In societies which are still modernizing across Africa, women have a heavy burden of changing the notions of women's place in the family, at the household level, and at work. [13]

11. Tong and Botts, *Feminist Thought*, 11–103.

12. Tong and Botts, *Feminist Thought*, 11–103.

13. Katrak, "Teaching Aidoo," 140–45.

Therefore, her presentation of feminism hardly reflects on an entirety of all contemporary feminist theories.

In fact, it is not easy to maintain a hard-line stance on these varieties of feminist thoughts since these attempts to explain woman's subordination intersect and at times join together. It is worth noting that approaches by feminists provide temporary and partial answers to questions that concern women's oppression, its causes, and plans for liberation. Largely, African women address female subordination with regard to cultural inhibitions and patriarchy. At the same time, according to the sociologists Stevi Jackson and Jackie Jones, feminist theory is not and has never been a static phenomenon. This is one reason why it has proven difficult to capture within classifications such as "liberal," "Marxist," or "radical."[14] Therefore, fixing hard-line categories could be said to be limiting or even misrepresenting.

Feminism in Western Europe and the United States emerged as early as the nineteenth century due to the rise of industrial enterprise, division of labor, and new emancipatory ideas in the aftermath of the French and American revolutions. However, looking at the effect of history on women from these two regions could shed some light on the same. Prior to the nineteenth century, most societies in Western Europe and the United States regarded women as subordinate to their male relatives, as women were excluded from equal access to education and participation in public life.

In most societies in Western Europe and the United States, the attitude towards women was that they were weak and delicate, incapable of being active in the public world of business and politics. According to Clifford, in 1792 Mary Wollstonecraft wrote a book titled *A Vindication of the Rights of Woman*, where she argued that men consider females as women rather than as human creatures. Later on, in 1833, in the United States, the Female Anti-Slavery society connected the oppression of slaves with the subordination of women.[15]

14. Jackson and Jones, *Contemporary Feminist Theories*, 2.

15. Clifford, *Introducing Feminist Theology*, 11.

Feminism is divided into first, second, and third waves primarily by virtue of periods. The first wave of feminism refers to the the mid-nineteenth century in Western Europe and North America and up to the 1920s (early twentieth century) when women in America obtained the right to vote. This kind of feminism was concerned with what Jóhannsdóttir calls the *de jure* (officially mandated) feminism whose main focus was on inequalities that were officially authorized fighting for equal civil rights, including the right of women to vote.[16] The second wave of feminism is traced back to the early 1960s, lasting until the late 1970s. It is associated with Euro-American women's advocacy for equal pay and equal rights in conjunction with the civil rights movement. It also brought into focus feminist studies as a new academic discipline. In most cases, this wave "fought for . . . increased freedom of women's sexual expression."[17] In that case, the second wave addressed a variety of issues which were not fully accomplished in the first wave such as "unofficial inequalities . . . official legal inequalities, sexuality, family, the workplace, and . . . reproductive rights."[18] Hence, in this wave of feminism, "Women demanded to be evaluated for their true worth inside and outside the home."[19]

In fact, it is in this Second Wave where radical feminists came into being. Mary Daly is one of the proponents of this kind of feminism. Radical feminists "criticized liberal feminists for closing their eyes to the fact that formal gender equality did in fact not reflect real equality."[20] Radical feminists are not necessarily against men; rather, they argue that "throughout history patriarchy has sought to oppress women." Their main emphasis is that

16. Jóhannsdóttir, "Patriarchy and the Subordination of Women," 6; cf. Chisale, "Patriarchy and Resistance."

17. Jóhannsdóttir, "Patriarchy and the Subordination of Women"; cf. Clifford, *Introducing Feminist Theology*, 12–16; Chisale, "Patriarchy and Resistance," 22.

18. Jóhannsdóttir, "Patriarchy and the Subordination of Women," 6–7.

19. Jóhannsdóttir, "Patriarchy and the Subordination of Women"; cf. Pillay, "Anglican Church," 61.

20. Jóhannsdóttir, "Patriarchy and the Subordination of Women," 8.

"women are universally oppressed and are passive."[21] In that case, one weakness of this strand of feminism is that its proponents distance themselves from men, believing that men are their enemies who control their reproductive power.[22] Liberal feminists had a different emphasis from that of radical feminists. Proponents, such as Betty Friedan, "campaign for equal opportunities for men and women."[23] Marxist feminism believes that capitalism is the main source of female oppression in society. For this strand of feminism, capitalism and patriarchy are the main focus of analysis as main agents of women's oppression. Yet, postmodern feminism stresses multiple human standpoints as being valid and of value. Proponents of postmodern feminism combine feminist and postmodern theory to argue in favor of diversity and multiple identities of women.[24]

In the third wave of feminism it became clear that European and Euro-American experience of discrimination was different from that of other racial and ethnic groups whose history included slavery and colonization. The third wave of feminism attends to differences among women from different parts of the world and is traceable to the 1975 international women's year.[25]

Moreover, there is the emerging fourth wave of feminism. This turns to technology as the main agent of propagating feminist ideas, especially the internet. Proponents of this wave "link fourth-wave feminism to technology, such as online social media and networks including Facebook, Twitter, Instagram, YouTube and Blogs."[26] In linking with these social media, they "argue that technology is used to campaign against gender injustice and other social systems that discriminate against women and other sexual minority groups . . . technology is used by feminists to challenge

21. Chisale, "Patriarchy and Resistance," 25.

22. Chisale, "Patriarchy and Resistance," 25.

23. Chisale, "Patriarchy and Resistance," 25.

24. Chisale, "Patriarchy and Resistance," 25.

25. Clifford, *Introducing Feminist Theology*, 12–16; cf. Chisale, "Patriarchy and Resistance," 23.

26. Chisale, "Patriarchy and Resistance," 24.

sexism or misogyny and refer to it as 'online feminism.'"[27] In this case, "Technology is used as a critical tool to communicate women's frustrations regarding gender equality and social injustice and it has spread the message to the girl child and boy child who have the privilege to growing up aware of feminism and the gender debate."[28]

In general, African feminists emphasize that they have unique experiences and concerns that are connected with their history and cultural context. Therefore, the third wave of feminism is relevant because attention is paid to difference. There are differences as to how the word "feminist" is viewed in the various social locations. In some places, the term is stigmatized as foreign. Studies by the theologian Elsa Tamez indicate that, in the 1970s, the word "feminist" in Latin America was stigmatized. Later, in the 1980s, the term, though not used or accepted in all circles, was accorded some tolerance, and "feminism" begun to be used to characterize theology from the standpoint of women. In the 1990s, feminist theology, women's theology, and theology from the viewpoint of women were used interchangeably. In the 1990s, the term "feminist" had been adopted and efforts were being made to destigmatize it.[29]

Similarly, in full view of the development of Latin America feminist hermeneutics, the term "feminist" will probably over time be met with more tolerance. In the Latin American case, the 1970's saw revolutionary struggles, military dictatorships coupled with political and theological militancy. Meanwhile, there was ideological polarisation so that feminists rejected religion and mistrusted women theologians, while women theologians rejected any feminist demands that were not linked to the overall economic liberation of the society.[30]

The terms "feminist theologians" and "woman theologians" may be differentiated because of the particular context and the

27. Chisale, "Patriarchy and Resistance," 24.
28. Chisale, "Patriarchy and Resistance," 24.
29. Tamez, "Latin American Feminist Hermeneutics," 83–86.
30. Tamez, "Latin American Feminist Hermeneutics," 79–86.

time. Chisale writes that "Globally, feminism is associated with women who have issues, or difficulty relating to men, or women who have failed in their marriages."[31] Women theology is a concept used by women who do not want to embrace the concept of feminism, those who do not see sexism as an issue. Chisale quotes the words of such a woman, Buchi Echemta, saying: "I have never called myself a feminist. Now if you choose to call me a feminist, that is your business; but I don't subscribe to the feminist idea that all men are brutal and repressive and we must reject them. Some of these men are my brothers and fathers and sons. Am I to reject them too?"[32] In this case, in most African societies, sexism is not an issue and most women would rather prefer to be called African women theologians instead of being African feminist theologians.

In accordance with the third wave of feminism, as previously noted, it is characterized by paying special attention to differences, so that it does not ignore or downplay them. At the same time, it does not use the differences to create barriers. It takes into account the many voices of women of color. It pays attention to the difference that social location makes in women's lives.

CONCLUSION

It is important to note that feminist theory does focus on four important themes, namely a commitment to ending the unjust subordination, recognition of women's oppression, an examination of what contributes to the maintenance of that oppression, and a futuristic vision of equality. These four themes bring us to a sharp focus on strengths of feminist theories; in that they can be applied to a broad range of issues. Also, feminist theories provide valuable critique of other theories and perspectives. However, some limitations of feminist theories include the claims that research and practice are emotionally charged and that there is an overemphasis on gender and power.

31. Chisale, "Patriarchy and Resistance," 30.
32. Chisale, "Patriarchy and Resistance," 30.

CHAPTER REVIEW

1. What is the meaning of the concept of feminism?

2. State the historical background of feminism.

3. What are the emphases of liberal feminists and socialist feminists?

4. When did feminism emerge in Western Europe and the United States? Why did feminism emerge in those societies?

5. List the various waves of feminism and describe the emphasis paid to each of them.

Chapter 3

THEOLOGY OF AFRICAN WOMEN

INTRODUCTION

THEOLOGY IN AFRICA CAN be done by the uneducated people; however, it is also a professional and systematic discipline in itself. The theologian James Cochrane believes that the role of people who are not trained should not be ignored because they produce incipient theologies from their experiences of faith in their daily lives. The theologies produced by untrained people provide contrasting experiences to the existing discourses which are both transformative for theological reflection in the academy and spiritually significant for the growth of individual Christians.[1]

In a similar vein, the theologian Gerald West introduces us to working theologies of people who are not academically trained. To him, poor and marginalized women have their own hermeneutics of resistance and survival; and in reading the Bible, they are able to construct their lived and working theologies. By their nature, these theologies may be precritical, scattered, and perhaps unsystematic; however, they draw on a range of ideas, rituals, symbols, and

---

1. Haddad, *African Women's Theologies*, 264.

readings which reflect their real lives. These theologies are theirs and reflect what they live by.[2]

Then we are also introduced to survival theologies. These theologies, according to the theologian Beverly Haddad, are theologies of the poor and the marginalized women who have not been trained in the academy. The subjugated expressions of these women's faith are found in assemblies of religious women and consist of survival theologies.[3]

Clearly, the three theologians have made an option for the poor and marginalized and, in order to take them seriously, they refer to their reflections and expressions as theologies. What is common from the three theologians, though they use different terms, is their use of the term "theologies" to denote what emerges from lay and untrained religious persons who express their faith. The theologians above are naming what is produced from a specific location, of the poor and the marginalized, though they do it variously.

Similarly, African women engage, reflect, and make known the expression of their faith multifariously. Their faith expressions that derive from their experiences stem from their relationship with God.[4] Hence, African women's theology demonstrates the concerns and priorities of African women theologians.[5]

In what follows, the theologian Steven B. Bevans captures this succinctly:

> What seems important is to conceive theology in terms of a constant dialogue between the people—who are the subjects of culture and cultural change and so have a preeminent place in the enterprise of seeking to understand Christian faith in a particular context—and the professional theologian who articulates, deepens and broadens the people's faith expression with his or her

2. Haddad, *African Women's Theologies*, 296.

3. Haddad, *African Women's Theologies*, 257.

4. Tappa, "Christ Event"; Hinga, "Jesus Christ"; Nasimiyu, "Christology and African Women's Experience."

5. Oduyoye, *Introducing African Women's Theology*, 10.

wider knowledge of the Christian tradition and perhaps, the articulation of faith in other contexts. What becomes clear as the context is taken seriously in theology is that, on the one hand, theology can never be understood as a finished product, produced by experts, that is merely delivered to a Christian community for its consumption.[6]

Following Bevans's above assertion, one can note that women in Africa are in constant dialogue with their culture, even as they seek to interpret and make sense of the Christian faith. This interpretation takes place within a specific milieu, which provides for the unique features of African women's theology. Indeed, owing to the pluralistic nature of feminist theology, and based on the fact that it is not a body developed systematically, women's actions and reflections as Christians can be called by a variety of names. This theology is called "womanist" by African American women, "women's liberation theology" by many in Latin America, and "women's theology" in Africa, while for others it is merely "feminist theology." Therefore, the main concern of this chapter is to examine the way these theologies portray themselves in the African continent. We examine the main themes, the current debates around women's experiences, and the way African women organize themselves.

MAIN THEMES, NORMS, AND SOURCES FOR AFRICAN WOMEN'S THEOLOGY

According to Oduyoye, (African) women do not accept that African men's theology should suffice for the entire faith community. There ought to be a study of African Christian theology in the women-centered key. This is to be understood as what highlights women as actors, agents, and thinkers.[7] Hence, as just said, the theology of African women demonstrates their concerns and priorities.

---

6. Bevans, *Models of Contextual Theology*, 18.

7. Oduyoye, *Introducing African Women's Theology*, 10.

African women theologians explore several themes. The theme of *community* is explored by many due to their sense of and responsibility for extended families and the respect accorded to ancestors. According to Oduyoye, to live in community is to do so in partnership and reciprocity. The ordering of the human community should not only be done by either the males or the females. In reciprocity within the community, women should not monopolize the servant role.[8] In general, Oduyoye insists that it is not enough to speak of community in Africa as an integral part of African culture, if the quality of community is not analyzed and deemed worthy in terms of promoting justice and support for women.

Moreover, according to Oduyoye, African women theologians explore the theme of *Christology* where Jesus is understood as both human and divine. Christology for them is not meant to analyze the nature of Christ, but rather to identify saving acts and cling onto them in hope of liberation. Christian women do turn to Jesus to find resources to transform the suffering and obstacles they meet as they deal with life-denying and life-threatening contexts of Africa.

They also focus on the theme of *ecclesiology*, where attention is paid to the household of God. The nurturing and upkeeping of the household of God becomes a central concern. *Eschatology* with reference to the resurrection of the body and the words of women are other themes looked into. The themes of hospitality and spirituality are also explored together with themes such as sacrifice, ecology, and missiology.[9]

Other themes explored by African women are the themes of *empowerment* and *liberation*. Liberation as a theme grants a voice to the voiceless, motivates to social change, and helps develop a new sense of responsibility and solidarity. Liberation from life-denying forces is sought out. By empowerment, African women theologians choose to understand power as "enabling power," empowerment that can be collective, can develop and increase so that

8. Oduyoye, "Feminist Theology," 178.

9. Oduyoye, *Introducing African Women's Theology*, 20.

31

all who participate in it are affirmed and strengthened. This is different from the power that is practiced in a dominant, hierarchical mode where power is exercised as "power over."

The above themes by African women theologians indicate their variety of commitments. At the same time, their emphasis is on praxis, on doing theology as an activity that is ongoing and rooted in praxis. It is from issues frequently encountered that they raise their theological concerns and hence the themes they attend to.

Sources for African women's theology are as follows: First, the *Bible*. Most of the African women theologians are keen churchwomen, several ordained into the Eucharist ministry while others are laywomen. For the African women theologians, the Bible is central in their theologizing. However, any interpretation of the Bible is unacceptable if it does harm to women, the vulnerable, and the voiceless.[10]

Second, another source is *stories*. Narrative theology prevails in both oral and written materials. Stories play a normative role in Africa in general and, therefore, African women accept stories as a source for theology.[11] A clear example is when Oduyoye adopts a popular Fante name, Anowa, whom she declares to be Africa's Ancestress. She uses ideas from folktales and myths of powerful women leaders within Asante and Yoruba culture. Oduyoye makes use of the literary ideas of two African writers, Ama Ata Aidoo and Ayi Kwei Armah, who write about a mythical woman by the name of Anowa. Both authors indicate that the mythical Anowa is a woman opposed to slavery and slave trade, and portray her as a symbol of all that is life-protecting and life-sustaining. For Oduyoye's purpose, Anowa represents a great Ancestress.[12] Third, *folklore and legends* provide another source. Here, African religiocultural heritage provides insights that are appropriated by the African women theologians. Written sources that are a useful source

10. Oduyoye, *Introducing African Women's Theology*, 12.

11. Oduyoye, *Introducing African Women's Theology*, 10.

12. Oduyoye, *Daughters of Anowa*, 8–10.

for African women's theology are articles and publications by the Circle.

Fourth, the *Christian feminist movement of the West* is another source for African women's theology. According to Kanyoro, "feminist methodology is used because it challenges cultural socialization and rejects the assumption that the roles of women and men have already been fixed, either by the creator or by the culture."[13] Feminist theology, after originating from the West, has developed because of African women's association with institutions, ideas and publications of the West.

An additional norm and source for African women's theology is African women's experience. Many African women theologians experience or have heard of the experiences of others on issues such as women laborers, sexual exploitation, oppressive hierarchical structures in the churches, oppressive customs, and marriage structure. African women's theology draws much from their context and experience since they do not write theology that is remote and removed from their daily living. They grant that there are unique experiences and insights that come from individuals in their contexts. However, this has raised debates, as shown below.

CURRENT DEBATES AROUND WOMEN'S EXPERIENCES

Commitments and characteristic assumptions that typify theological reflection labeled feminist very often embrace appeals to women's experience. But over the years, a notion of "women's experience" as an alternative source for knowledge has been questioned. This is so because it is related to the claims of a female nature being one, universal, and historically stable. In fact, there is a profound critique of the supposed universal nature of "woman"; instead there is a claim that what we label as woman already has connotations attached to it, created by society for its female species.

---

13. Kanyoro, "Engendered Communal Theology," 168.

According to Eriksson, "it is not always clear whether the experience referred to in the feminist discourse is an 'inner experience' or a wider notion 'life or general experience'. . . . Women's experience is both a complex and troublesome category in feminist theory; when used, it needs to be examined and explicated."[14] As per theologian Sheila Davaney, women's experience as the norm arose because of its privileged character. This privilege arises from claims about women's status and ontological nature coupled with women's historical experience of oppression.[15]

Pamela Dickey Young writes that women's experience is a source and norm of feminist theology and can include women's bodily experience, women's historical experience, women's socialized experience, or even women's feminist experiences. Women's experience is held on to as a well-functioning norm because many women are dissatisfied with contemporary theology. Rather than finding Christian theology liberating, many women continue to experience oppression from it. In Christian theology, many women have been non-persons when seen in terms of liberation theologians.[16]

It is unrealistic to eliminate women's experiences wholesale because both women and men experience the world as gendered beings. In general, there is a historical entity in women's experience. Yet, traditionally, the use of the "women's experience" category has often denied the recognition that there are other forms of oppression other than gender. This is because the emphasis on the commonality of women's experience easily conceals racial and class differences among women. It renders invisible and absorbs the lives of the varieties of women in the world. In essence, there is a need for a more localized interpretation of women's experience that traces the historically particular situations of the women concerned.

---

14. Eriksson, *Meaning of Gender*, 46.

15. Davaney, "Continuing the Story," 200.

16. Yong, *Feminist Theology*, 60–62.

HOW AFRICAN WOMEN THEOLOGIANS ORGANIZE THEMSELVES

Currently, the organization of African women theologians is based upon two institutions: EATWOT and the Circle of Concerned African Women Theologians (CCAWT). In this section we will discuss the two women organizations and the way women organize themselves within these organizations.

EATWOT and Its Women Commission

In 1976, theologians gathered from different third world countries in Tanzania for the consultations titled "The Ecumenical Dialogue of Third World Theologians." They formed the Ecumenical Association of Third World Theologians, hereafter referred to as EATWOT, and of which the EATWOT women's commission is an integral part. Therefore this gathering was one of the major attempts of third world women to unite and articulate theology together.

EATWOT is a forum for the different varieties of third world theologies, to enable Christians of the third world to explain their understanding of revelation in the midst of what they face daily. It is an organization of theologians from Asia, Africa, Latin America, and some other areas considered parts of the third world. In general, the goal of EATWOT is the continuous development of Christian theologies of the third world to serve the commission of the church in the world, and to proclaim the new humanity in Christ in the struggle for a just society.

The use of the title EATWOT has been contested on grounds that "third world" denotes a derogatory flavor. The theologian Per Frostin notes: "Others argue that, the concepts of first world and third world are too crude to be useful as analytical tools."[17] To others, the term "third world" is suspect, since it connotes third place in a hierarchy of worlds. Some even speak of a fourth world.

17. Frostin, *Luther's Two Kingdoms*, 100.

According to King, "the term 'fourth world' is understood to refer to those who lead third world lives in the first world countries for example members of specific minorities and aboriginal people"[18] Therefore, the judgement on who falls first, second, and third may be argued against since, if the factor of material affluence should decide the divisions of this one world, then there are the materially affluent in what has been called the "third world," and there are the materially deprived present in what has been called "first world." In other words, there is a "third world" in the first world and vice versa.

In general, it can be said that the world is one and the divisions of first, second, third, and fourth are based on a division of economic and material affluence, therefore elevating economics above politics, religion, ethics, and the social dimension of life. This division can be said to be unreal because there is only one world.

Although there may be valid reservations for the usage of the term "third world," reference is made to it in this book because EATWOT members insist that the term is an account of the actual distribution of power. According to Frostin, EATWOT argues that there is a third world, since these countries have had similar experiences of which account should be taken in the task of theologising. Specifically, the third world is constituted by a common experience, [the experience of a commonality] that is the bitter fruit of oppression.[19] Frostin further suggests that it is not the term EATWOT that is derogatory, but the reality which is accounted for by the term.

African feminist theologians note how the study of the traditional religions and the promotion of indigenous spirituality are at the fore within EATWOT. African feminist theologians are interested in this indigenous spirituality since they note an African attempt to allow for various manifestations of spirituality by African women. At the same time, women's participation in prophetic roles that once characterized tribal tradition is taken seriously.

18. King, *Feminist Theology*, 2.

19. Frostin, *Luther's Two Kingdoms*, 100.

Therefore, EATWOT is recognized as a significant step in African theology. In 1986 in Oaxtapec, Mexico, EATWOT's women commission was launched and its goal was to focus on the life and work of women in the church. Its commission is to analyze women's oppression because of their sex, and to examine the demeaning construction of gender in both church and society. EATWOT women's commission is an arena for interreligious dialogue since African Traditional Religion is regarded as one of the sources of African theology. This is important for African women theologians who take note of the uncompromisingly male monotheistic faiths at the same time as they see conditions in society that remain male-dominated.

The Circle of Concerned African Women Theologians (CCAWT)

Having discussed EATWOT, an initiative of third world theologians towards unity in articulating theology, we now move towards the Circle of Concerned African Women Theologians. In September 1989, the Circle was founded in Accra, Ghana. The Circle was inaugurated in order to facilitate the writing, research, and publication by a Pan-African multireligious and multiracial network of women. The Circle is a contemporary network of women from across Africa, some of whom live outside Africa. It is a voluntary movement, whose work often takes place within regional meetings. Within the Circle is the open acknowledgement and appreciation of differences, therefore, there is a focus to work hand in hand, and not in division or strife.[20]

The Circle places emphasis on the impact of religion and culture upon African women. According to Hinga, the Circle is concerned with voicing protests against sexism and its roots in religion and culture.[21] The Circle seeks to develop women's

20. Togarasei, "Legacy of Circle Women's Engagement."

21. Hinga, "Between Colonialism," 31; cf. Togarasei, "Legacy of Circle Women's Engagement."

theological contribution in churches, schools, colleges, universities, and society, and therefore be agents of change in both customary and modern legislation.

The Circle members dialogue with their male counterparts in many areas. These common areas include poverty, racism, and cultural, social, ethnic, and political problems. Most of the circle founders are members of EATWOT. Further, the Circle members present a "two-winged" theology. This theology asserts a relationship with African men. In this theology, women work in cooperation with men of good will for the reconstruction of a cultural and religious praxis of sexual equality. But this theology also emphasizes the necessity of critiquing culture and religion from the perspective of "Christ as the norm for the fullness of the human being."[22] Participants of the Circle regard Oduyoye as the queen mother of the movement.[23]

CONCLUSION

In describing "theology from the perspective of African women," we note that genuine theologizing by women involves reflections on the conceptions of God in their daily lives and needs in the church. Therefore, theology may be done by those women who are not formally educated, who express theology through spontaneous poetic lyrics, songs, and prayers. It is also done at a formal level by women who are Sunday school teachers and guidance counselors. At the same time, it can also be done at an academic level.[24] Consequently, African women theologians organize themselves variously in order to articulate their interests as a group, to get mentorship from each other, and to share their experiences. Many of their reflections have been articulated in books sponsored by the circle of African women theologians, making these accessible to a wider audience.

22. Oduyoye, *Who will Roll the Stone Away?*, 27; cf. Togarasei, "Legacy of Circle Women's Engagement," 9.

23. Pemberton, *Circle Thinking*, 63.

24. Amoah, "Theology from the Perspective," 1.

CHAPTER REVIEW

1. Elaborate on the main themes explored by African women theologians in their theologies.

2. Discuss the sources of African women's theology.

3. How do African women theologians organize themselves?

Chapter 4

WOMEN WITHIN THE AFRICAN
TRADITIONAL RELIGION

INTRODUCTION

AFRICAN THEOLOGIANS MAINTAIN THAT the view of Africa, its peoples, and their culture by most missionaries was largely negative. According to Kwame Bediako, this view resounded with Europe's first impressions of Africa and its people, which resulted from the contact owing to slave trade. Therefore, it is not surprising that because of this perception, missionaries saw Africans as being in the very depths of ignorant superstition.[1]

According to Susannah Herzel, the coming of Christianity robbed women of the consideration which they had. Before Christianity and colonialism came to Africa, African women had a considerable status, having various gifts such as healings, prophecy, and exorcisms. Women exercised these gifts voluntarily in the their societies, including in the African religion which they believed and practiced.[2] It was very significant to note them being

1. Bediako, *Theology and Identity*, 227.

2. Herzel, *Voice for Women*, 68; cf. Maseno and Owojaiye, "African Women and Revival," 31.

involved in prophetic roles within the African indigenous religion. The high regard for prophecy in Africa then and today makes the involvement of women one of the significant roles. In Africa, God speaks through people; hence, the voice of God by a prophet is automatically considered to be the voice of the people. Therefore, through their involvement in various gifts, African women in the indigenous religion were automatically in places of leadership through the roles they assumed.[3]

Though scholars disagree on the place of women in traditional African societies, there is at least a consensus that the place of women in Africa's religious tradition was significant. According to Musa Dube, women in African societies were not put aside; rather, they held prominent religious positions.[4] However, this was not the case after the coming of Christianity and the colonizers. After the coming of Christianity and the colonizers, things changed. The patriarchal attitude of the colonizers was imposed because it was embedded in the religion (Christianity) they propagated. The British governor in the colony was an Anglican, representing the monarch of Britain, who was also the head of the Anglican Church. The uncompromising male monotheistic faith, with its many references to when Christianity came to Africa, went with the sidelining of women in leadership within Christianity.

Another issue that had negative effects on the status of women after the coming of Christianity and the colonizers was that of formal education. Formal education hardly favored the training of both male and female. It favored the training of males for the church. Since this kind of education favored the training of males for the church and the colonial offices, African females were rarely included. The missionary religion (Christianity) contrary to the indigenous African religion endorsed the training of African males, who in turn assumed and enforced a strictly patriarchal view of the church and in the use of the Bible. According to Hinga, the distinct history of Africans is a history that is marked by colonialism,

---

3. Herzel, *Voice for Women*, 67–69; cf. Maseno and Owojaiye, "African Women and Revival," 31–32.

4. Dube, "Go Therefore and Make Disciples," 226.

therefore the cultural context from which African women theologians speak is distinct. There is a decisively ambiguous impact of Christianity in the lives of African women. To her, Christianity participated in the oppression of women, since it has functioned to legitimize colonialism, racism, and sexism.[5] Therefore, we can just say that the major role played by Christianity in Africa mainly endorsed patriarchy and an androcentric mindset among people.

More often than not, the missionaries and the churches had derogatory names for the gifts which women had. For example, they called African women's gifts of healing, prophecy, and exorcism as "strange gifts." Calling them with these derogatory names served to alienate all women who exercised the so-called strange gifts, according them the status of outcasts, considering them as people who not worthy of respect in society. As it can clearly be noted, African indigenous religion allowed women to freely exercise their spirituality, unlike the missionary Christianity and the colonizers who hindered them of their spiritual visibility. However, Maseno and Owojaiye contend that "Accommodating the 'strange gifts' of African women may have reduced the alternative schismatic tendencies that resulted in the formation of African Independent Churches."[6] A male majority in churches where women experienced the colonial and missionary dominations caused them to think of an alternative African way to communicate with God. Thus, we clearly note that a considerable number of independent churches in Africa have been started by women as a reaction to the mainstream Christianity.[7]

As we have just said above, the concern of both Christianity and the colonial culture was mainly to legitimize patriarchy in Africa. The major function of patriarchy is to articulate dualisms and validate relations of domination and subordination; as a result, the hierarchical order of society emerges and provides power to men. This is what came into view when Christianity entered the sub-Saharan region. The coming of sub-Saharan Christianity

5. Hinga, "Between Colonialism and Inculturation," 36.

6. Maseno and Owojaiye, "African Women and Revival," 32.

7. Herzel, *Voice for Women*, 68.

among the African women theologians and the feminist movement in the West, it is important to elaborate on feminism and feminist theology.

According to Herzel, research by people such as John Mbiti, David Barratt seems to confirm the sacramental ministry of women as prophetesses, dating back to very early times. Accordingly, a considerable number of independent churches in Africa have been started by women. Where in parts of Africa women assume positions of leadership in religious movements, it is often a reassertion of the prophetic role which once characterized their tribal religion. In sum we could say that prophecy was a significant role of women in African religions. On the other hand, since women gifts were branded "strange," much was missed.

Enthusiasm has always marked female emancipation. According to Herzel, the Western male horror of this phenomenon ensured that the African structures established by Western churches excluded women in leadership ranks. In African prophetic movements, Mbiti maintains, women found extraordinary and quite exceptional ministries and leadership. To him, in Africa the prophet or prophetess movements remain a deliberate attempt by traditional Africans to make Western Christianity meaningful.

Oyeronke Olajubu, in her work "A Socio-cultural Analysis of Yoruba Women and the Re-Imaging Christianity," notes that the Yoruba who are occupants of the Southwestern part of Nigeria and some part of the republic of Benin, practice many religions such as Christianity, Islam, Yoruba religion, the New Age movement, and mystic groups. To her, women constitute a majority of membership of these religions. Women play leadership roles in Yoruba religion, owing to the holistic paradigms of Yoruba religion which provides empowerment for both male and females alike.

Olajubu maintains that women in Yoruba religion are central where rituals are concerned. Women significantly influence and modulate ritual practices. Women therefore achieve through these innovations the creation of alternative spaces and axes of power evaluation, the group motif and prioritizing the experienced above the prescriptive. According to Olajubu, roles played by female and

was closely intertwined with the colonial regimes. According to Oduyoye, the arrival of Western Christianity was an attack on the African way of life as it collaborated with colonial administration, therefore propagating colonial violence.[8]

Dube, in her introduction to post-colonial theories, states that studies of imperialism show factors that have motivated and justified imperialism: God, glory, and gold. Some may term these as power, moral responsibility and economic interests.[9] In effect, to achieve these goals, colonial governments collaborated with the missionaries, and there was a propagation and maintenance of imperial violence. In so doing, they maintained a form of exploitation. According to Dube, this exploitation denied (African) women and men their political, cultural, and economic autonomy by imposing its systems of power for its own benefit.[10]

Therefore, as understood by Oduyoye, "[African women] have to contend however with the fact that western Christian culture and patriarchal ideology have seeped in, to enhance the power of men or to endow men with power where they had none, while suppressing aspects of African culture that are favourable to women."[11] In general, the interaction of African women with Western Christianity that collaborated with colonial powers left them exploited, exposed to terrible forms of violence and perpetual dependency.

Theology is God-talk. From this understanding, we can say that it is not possible to talk about an "emergence of African women theologians" as something recent. Nevertheless, through speeches, songs, dance, stories, and prayers, African women were able to express their thoughts and conceptualization of who God is. Indeed, it is important to note that African women do theology in Africa at different levels. African women had, over time, remained unrepresented in formal theological training, and as the theologian John Parratt puts it, there was a paucity of theologically

8. Oduyoye, *Introducing African Women's Theology*, 28.

9. Dube, *Postcolonial Feminist Interpretation*, 47.

10. Dube, *Postcolonial Feminist Interpretation*, 29.

11. Oduyoye, *Introducing African Women's Theology*, 28.

trained women.[12] Reasons that explain why African women would not access formal theological training include, first, for many African women, there was a shortage of employment possibilities for theologically trained women. According to Musimbi Kanyoro, it has been noted that the church rarely makes use of its African women who are trained theologians. Many are assigned to work within educational institutions or with parachurch organizations.[13]

Second, many women were hindered from pursuing theological training owing to the lack of church sponsorship and financial constraints. Theological training in Africa was often provided at a denominational level with an aim of having ordained staff for their respective churches. However, ordination of women was unheard of. Therefore, the African males' language about God dominated, and men become self-appointed spokespersons for women and children. The resonance of voices of women academicians and those in the community at large makes a strong case that for women in Africa, theology is an activity rooted in praxis. There is an emphasis on doing theology and not just writing it.

Theologian Rosemary Ruether states that

> all inherited culture has been male biased and sexist, however, all significant works of culture have not only legitimised sexism. They have done something else. They have been responding to the fears of death, estrangement, oppression . . . and the liberation of humanity. Although they have articulated this response in male terms, women can discover this critical element in male culture and transform it, so that it says things it has never said before.[14]

For African women theologians to transform male culture, they cannot mimic the voices of their male counterparts. Instead, they have to break the silence and demand to speak for themselves. Their voices should result from a deconstruction of male dominated

12. Parratt, *Reinventing Christianity*, 5.

13. Oduyoye and Kanyoro, *Will to Arise*, 5; Maponda, "Impact of the Circle."

14. Ruether, *Mary*, 39.

reality to an effort to reconstruct reality in more hur this reason, it can be said that they would be mor reality. Despite the numerous challenges and obsta African women theologians, they have "emerged" in they have broken the spell of inevitability cast by the them.

AFRICAN WOMEN THEOLOGIANS AND

African women theologians began utilizing femini only in the late eighties. The theologian Ursula Ki "Feminist theology anywhere, whether in the First world, would never have come about without wom to theological education up to the highest academi cording to Parratt, the earliest sustained exposition (to come from an African woman (Mercy Oduyoye) book titled *Hearing and Knowing*.[16] A reason for th been previously discussed on the formal theologic African women.

The feminist critique developed by Western fe imposed upon African women theologians. Rathe selves stress the agency of their own struggle on the Therefore, it is not possible to isolate African wo critique as unaffected by the wider feminist theol West. There has been a sharing and an interaction place and enabled African women theologians to a oppression in society and in the church, among oth cordingly, they share in the fact that academic Chri theology incorporates feminist theories developed logical institutions.[17] Owing to the relation of fem

15. King, *Feminist Theology*, 5.

16. Parratt, *Reinventing Christianity*, 51.

17. Clifford, *Introducing Feminist Theology*, 5.

male persona in mythical narratives have profound implications for the expected roles of females and males in society. Yoruba cosmological accounts thus prescribe and entrench complementary gender relations that find expressions in the religious interactions of men and women as well as in their relations in the polity. Thus female leadership roles and access to power in religion are anchored on divine provisions that are validated by these cosmological narratives.[18]

Whereas in Yoruba religion the obvious area of authority in the polity is in the custody of men, women control the base of men's public authority through mystical powers. An example of such mystical powers is the IYA MI group. This is a group of powerful women with powers delegated to them by *Olodumare*, the creator. These women wield a lot of power in an informal and often invisible but effectual way. It is to be noted that the visible cannot stand save the invisible base of these women.

The base of Yoruba worldview is the cosmological myth, which postulates that *Olodumare* created and equipped both male and female with different powers and areas of specializations. *Olodumare* preferred cooperation between the female and the male in the resolve of tension that would arise out of the daily enterprise of living. Olajubu further maintains that in Yoruba religion, women are the ones who sustain and transmit religious traditions. Clearly, in Yoruba religion, myths and oral narratives which serve as the people's storehouse of philosophy show gender interdependency, as opposed to oppression of women by men. Thus, the prevalent domination of women by men is untenable in religious traditions in Yoruba land.

To her, through group formation, women in Yoruba religion profess to be able to effect change in society as a collective endeavor. This is known as *egbe* among the Yoruba. Spiritually, the *egbe* is a middle ground between the unseen spiritual forces and human gifts and connections of communication with the unseen forces. Through these groups, women participate in activities which touch upon both the social and spiritual dimensions. Through these

18. Olajubu, "Socio-cultural Analysis."

47

groups women support each other during weddings, funerals, bereavement, and in ceremonies of children. However, the coming of Christianity disrupted the social framework of Yoruba gender relations significantly. This disruption was due to Western education and the distinction between the private and the public sector. The distinction created arenas that were not there previously.

In sum, Olajubu accentuates the pivotal role of women in Yoruba religion. These women participate in very important activities which touch upon both the social and spiritual dimensions of the community. More to the point, they influence the unseen/spiritual realms, which is very significant and has a direct bearing on the seen/physical realm

Another scholar who lends credence to the whole area of women in African Traditional Religion is John Mbiti in his article "The Role of Women in African Traditional Religion." Here, Mbiti examines the place and role of women according to African religion. His paper focuses on three areas: mythology, proverbs, and prayers. In the area of mythology, we are confronted with the picture of women in the early state of human existence. We shall dwell on two areas: those of mythology and proverbs, as competently articulated by Mbiti.

WOMEN IN AFRICAN MYTHOLOGY

A large number of myths are found in Africa. Every African people (tribe) has its own body of myths, stories, legends, and oral history. We want to concentrate here mainly on the myths dealing with the origin of human beings because women are featured very prominently in these myths. Some myths speak about an original Mother of mankind from whom all people originated. The Ibibio (of Nigeria) say that human beings came from the divinity *Obumo*, who was the son of the mother-divinity *Eka-Abassi*. It is told in Eastern Africa about a virgin woman *Ekao*, who fell on earth from the sky and bore a son; the son got married to another woman and founded human society.

was closely intertwined with the colonial regimes. According to Oduyoye, the arrival of Western Christianity was an attack on the African way of life as it collaborated with colonial administration, therefore propagating colonial violence.[8]

Dube, in her introduction to post-colonial theories, states that studies of imperialism show factors that have motivated and justified imperialism: God, glory, and gold. Some may term these as power, moral responsibility and economic interests.[9] In effect, to achieve these goals, colonial governments collaborated with the missionaries, and there was a propagation and maintenance of imperial violence. In so doing, they maintained a form of exploitation. According to Dube, this exploitation denied (African) women and men their political, cultural, and economic autonomy by imposing its systems of power for its own benefit.[10]

Therefore, as understood by Oduyoye, "[African women] have to contend however with the fact that western Christian culture and patriarchal ideology have seeped in, to enhance the power of men or to endow men with power where they had none, while suppressing aspects of African culture that are favourable to women."[11] In general, the interaction of African women with Western Christianity that collaborated with colonial powers left them exploited, exposed to terrible forms of violence and perpetual dependency.

Theology is God-talk. From this understanding, we can say that it is not possible to talk about an "emergence of African women theologians" as something recent. Nevertheless, through speeches, songs, dance, stories, and prayers, African women were able to express their thoughts and conceptualization of who God is. Indeed, it is important to note that African women do theology in Africa at different levels. African women had, over time, remained unrepresented in formal theological training, and as the theologian John Parratt puts it, there was a paucity of theologically

8. Oduyoye, *Introducing African Women's Theology*, 28.

9. Dube, *Postcolonial Feminist Interpretation*, 47.

10. Dube, *Postcolonial Feminist Interpretation*, 29.

11. Oduyoye, *Introducing African Women's Theology*, 28.

trained women.[12] Reasons that explain why African women would not access formal theological training include, first, for many African women, there was a shortage of employment possibilities for theologically trained women. According to Musimbi Kanyoro, it has been noted that the church rarely makes use of its African women who are trained theologians. Many are assigned to work within educational institutions or with parachurch organizations.[13]

Second, many women were hindered from pursuing theological training owing to the lack of church sponsorship and financial constraints. Theological training in Africa was often provided at a denominational level with an aim of having ordained staff for their respective churches. However, ordination of women was unheard of. Therefore, the African males' language about God dominated, and men become self-appointed spokespersons for women and children. The resonance of voices of women academicians and those in the community at large makes a strong case that for women in Africa, theology is an activity rooted in praxis. There is an emphasis on doing theology and not just writing it.

Theologian Rosemary Ruether states that

> all inherited culture has been male biased and sexist, however, all significant works of culture have not only legitimised sexism. They have done something else. They have been responding to the fears of death, estrangement, oppression . . . and the liberation of humanity. Although they have articulated this response in male terms, women can discover this critical element in male culture and transform it, so that it says things it has never said before.[14]

For African women theologians to transform male culture, they cannot mimic the voices of their male counterparts. Instead, they have to break the silence and demand to speak for themselves. Their voices should result from a deconstruction of male dominated

12. Parratt, *Reinventing Christianity*, 5.

13. Oduyoye and Kanyoro, *Will to Arise*, 5; Maponda, "Impact of the Circle."

14. Ruether, *Mary*, 39.

reality to an effort to reconstruct reality in more human terms. For this reason, it can be said that they would be more in tune with reality. Despite the numerous challenges and obstacles that faced African women theologians, they have "emerged" in the sense that they have broken the spell of inevitability cast by the males around them.

AFRICAN WOMEN THEOLOGIANS AND FEMINISM

African women theologians began utilizing feminist approaches only in the late eighties. The theologian Ursula King stated that "Feminist theology anywhere, whether in the First or the Third world, would never have come about without women's full access to theological education up to the highest academic level."[15] According to Parratt, the earliest sustained exposition (on feminism) to come from an African woman (Mercy Oduyoye) was Oduyoye's book titled *Hearing and Knowing*.[16] A reason for this is what has been previously discussed on the formal theological training of African women.

The feminist critique developed by Western feminists is not imposed upon African women theologians. Rather, they themselves stress the agency of their own struggle on their own terms. Therefore, it is not possible to isolate African women feminist critique as unaffected by the wider feminist theology from the West. There has been a sharing and an interaction that has taken place and enabled African women theologians to analyze female oppression in society and in the church, among other things. Accordingly, they share in the fact that academic Christian feminist theology incorporates feminist theories developed outside theological institutions.[17] Owing to the relation of feminist critique

15. King, *Feminist Theology*, 5.
16. Parratt, *Reinventing Christianity*, 51.
17. Clifford, *Introducing Feminist Theology*, 5.

among the African women theologians and the feminist movement in the West, it is important to elaborate on feminism and feminist theology.

According to Herzel, research by people such as John Mbiti, David Barratt seems to confirm the sacramental ministry of women as prophetesses, dating back to very early times. Accordingly, a considerable number of independent churches in Africa have been started by women. Where in parts of Africa women assume positions of leadership in religious movements, it is often a reassertion of the prophetic role which once characterized their tribal religion. In sum we could say that prophecy was a significant role of women in African religions. On the other hand, since women gifts were branded "strange," much was missed.

Enthusiasm has always marked female emancipation. According to Herzel, the Western male horror of this phenomenon ensured that the African structures established by Western churches excluded women in leadership ranks. In African prophetic movements, Mbiti maintains, women found extraordinary and quite exceptional ministries and leadership. To him, in Africa the prophet or prophetess movements remain a deliberate attempt by traditional Africans to make Western Christianity meaningful.

Oyeronke Olajubu, in her work "A Socio-cultural Analysis of Yoruba Women and the Re-Imaging Christianity," notes that the Yoruba who are occupants of the Southwestern part of Nigeria and some part of the republic of Benin, practice many religions such as Christianity, Islam, Yoruba religion, the New Age movement, and mystic groups. To her, women constitute a majority of membership of these religions. Women play leadership roles in Yoruba religion, owing to the holistic paradigms of Yoruba religion which provides empowerment for both male and females alike.

Olajubu maintains that women in Yoruba religion are central where rituals are concerned. Women significantly influence and modulate ritual practices. Women therefore achieve through these innovations the creation of alternative spaces and axes of power evaluation, the group motif and prioritizing the experienced above the prescriptive. According to Olajubu, roles played by female and male persona in mythical narratives have profound implications for the expected roles of females and males in society. Yoruba cosmological accounts thus prescribe and entrench complementary gender relations that find expressions in the religious interactions of men and women as well as in their relations in the polity. Thus female leadership roles and access to power in religion are anchored on divine provisions that are validated by these cosmological narratives.[18]

Whereas in Yoruba religion the obvious area of authority in the polity is in the custody of men, women control the base of men's public authority through mystical powers. An example of such mystical powers is the IYA MI group. This is a group of powerful women with powers delegated to them by *Olodumare*, the creator. These women wield a lot of power in an informal and often invisible but effectual way. It is to be noted that the visible cannot stand save the invisible base of these women.

The base of Yoruba worldview is the cosmological myth, which postulates that *Olodumare* created and equipped both male and female with different powers and areas of specializations. *Olodumare* preferred cooperation between the female and the male in the resolve of tension that would arise out of the daily enterprise of living. Olajubu further maintains that in Yoruba religion, women are the ones who sustain and transmit religious traditions. Clearly, in Yoruba religion, myths and oral narratives which serve as the people's storehouse of philosophy show gender interdependency, as opposed to oppression of women by men. Thus, the prevalent domination of women by men is untenable in religious traditions in Yoruba land.

To her, through group formation, women in Yoruba religion profess to be able to effect change in society as a collective endeavor. This is known as *egbe* among the Yoruba. Spiritually, the *egbe* is a middle ground between the unseen spiritual forces and human gifts and connections of communication with the unseen forces. Through these groups, women participate in activities which touch upon both the social and spiritual dimensions. Through these

18. Olajubu, "Socio-cultural Analysis."

groups women support each other during weddings, funerals, bereavement, and in ceremonies of children. However, the coming of Christianity disrupted the social framework of Yoruba gender relations significantly. This disruption was due to Western education and the distinction between the private and the public sector. The distinction created arenas that were not there previously.

In sum, Olajubu accentuates the pivotal role of women in Yoruba religion. These women participate in very important activities which touch upon both the social and spiritual dimensions of the community. More to the point, they influence the unseen/spiritual realms, which is very significant and has a direct bearing on the seen/physical realm

Another scholar who lends credence to the whole area of women in African Traditional Religion is John Mbiti in his article "The Role of Women in African Traditional Religion." Here, Mbiti examines the place and role of women according to African religion. His paper focuses on three areas: mythology, proverbs, and prayers. In the area of mythology, we are confronted with the picture of women in the early state of human existence. We shall dwell on two areas: those of mythology and proverbs, as competently articulated by Mbiti.

WOMEN IN AFRICAN MYTHOLOGY

A large number of myths are found in Africa. Every African people (tribe) has its own body of myths, stories, legends, and oral history. We want to concentrate here mainly on the myths dealing with the origin of human beings because women are featured very prominently in these myths. Some myths speak about an original Mother of mankind from whom all people originated. The Ibibio (of Nigeria) say that human beings came from the divinity *Obumo*, who was the son of the mother-divinity *Eka-Abassi*. It is told in Eastern Africa about a virgin woman *Ekao*, who fell on earth from the sky and bore a son; the son got married to another woman and founded human society.

The main idea here is to link human life directly to God through the woman. She is created by God, and in turn becomes the instrument of human life. She rightly becomes the one who passes on life. This is well-illustrated in a myth of the Tutsi (of Rwanda). They tell that the original pair of human beings was in paradise. However, both the man and the woman were sterile and could not bear children. So they begged God to help them. God mixed clay with saliva and formed a small human figure. He instructed the woman to put the figure into a pot and keep it there for nine months. Every day the woman had to pour milk into the pot, mornings and evenings. She was to take out the figure only when it had grown limbs. So she followed these instructions, and after nine months she pulled out what had now become a human being. This myth describes the obedience of the woman and the diligence she manifests to daily keep the instructions given to her. Her dedication results in procreation.

God made other human beings according to this method, and these later increased on the earth. The pot is here a symbol of the womb of a mother, in which a baby takes shape and after nine months is born. The woman shares directly with God, in a personal way, the secrets and mysteries of life and birth. This role of the woman in sharing the mysteries of life started already in the mythological time.

In other myths of man's origin, the woman is always or nearly always mentioned. In many cases, even the name of the first woman is given in the myths, and some myths mention only the name of the woman and not of the man. A lot of myths say that the first human pair was lowered by God from the sky to the ground (earth), such as the myths of the Akamba, Turkana, Luo, Luhyia, and others in Kenya.

In a few myths, it is told that the woman was made by God out of the man's body, or after the man had been made. Perhaps behind these myths is the wish and practice on the part of males to dominate women. For example, the Kwotto (of Nigeria) say that God made the first human beings out of the earth (soil). God made (created) first the husband, and when God had become tired, God then made the wife (woman), who turned out to be weaker than her husband. This worldview already posits the woman as the lesser being contributing to her disadvantage in the community.

The life of the first human beings is generally depicted as having been in a form of paradise. God provided for them; in some cases, they lived in the sky (heaven) with God or on earth with them; God gave them one of the three important gifts: immortality, resurrection (if they died), or rejuvenation (if they grew old). However, this paradise got lost, the earth and heaven separated, God went to live up in heaven while men lived on the earth, the three gifts got lost, and in their place came diseases, suffering, and death.

Some myths speak of a test which God put to the original people. They failed. So the misfortunes of death and suffering, of God's separation from men, came about. Other myths explain that this occurred as a result of jealousies and quarrels within human families. Still in other myths, the cause originated from animals, like the hyena which, being (always) hungry, sought and ate the leather rope that had united heaven (sky) and earth.

However, some myths put the blame on the women. Thus, for example, it was a woman who in Ashanti myths (of Ghana), while pounding *fufu* (national food), went on knocking against God who lived in the sky. So God decided to go higher up. The good woman instructed her children that they should use a mortar to construct a tower, piling it up one mortar on top of the other. The tower became tall, almost reaching God. However, it left a small space that could be filled with only a single mortar; Since the children had no more mortar to fill the space, their mother told them they should take the bottom-most mortar and fill the gap. As soon as they removed the bottom-most mortar, the whole tower fell down and took the lives of many people.

In one of the Pygmy (*Bambuti*) myths, it is told that God gave the first people one rule: they could eat the fruits of all the trees, except from one tree. The people observed this regulation, awaiting a pregnant woman overcome by desire, and who tirelessly insisted on her husband to get the prohibited fruit for her. Finally, he crept secretly into the forest, picked the fruit, and brought it to her. However, the moon was watching all this and went and reported it to God. God became very angry and sent death to the people as punishment.

Despite the blames directed to the woman in the above myths for the bad luck that faced human beings, yet she is clearly neither the main nor the only offender. Indeed, the myths that put the blame on her are proportionally few. They indicate that she shares in the cause and effect of suffering, misfortune, and death in the world. She is a human being like men and children. She is also graced with the mysteries of life at the other end—just as she shares in the mysteries of life's beginning, so she shares in life's end.

WOMEN IN AFRICAN PROVERBS

Proverbs are significantly more plentiful than myths. These are very forceful in community because they contribute a lot of opinions, experiences, ideas, knowledge, reflections, observations, and even worldviews, by using just a few words.[19] Obododimma, quoting the words of Monye, writes: "*When people use proverbs there is always some relationship between two situations being compared: the proverb statement and its referent in the social context. It is this concatenateness between the human experience and another which gives proverbs their relevance.*"[20] In order to illustrate this analogical functions of the proverbs, we shall here quote only a few of them and try to capture what they intend to portray in positive and negative ways.

Positively, women are depicted as being extremely valuable in the sight of society. Their value is not only based on their ability to give birth to new life, but also their ability to cherish, take care of, and provide warmth for that life, since God has made that their bodies be mediums for the whole human life to pass through. The following proverbs bring these points out clearly: "Wives and oxen

19. Sibanda, "Analysis of the Significance of Myths."

20. Obododimma, "Semantics of Female Devaluation," 90 (italics in original).

have no friends." This proverb indicates the value of the wife over any other animal. Someone's wife cannot be provided to another, even to the best friend of her husband. For that reason, another proverb reminds us that "A woman must not be killed." Since life passes through her, the woman is regarded as the mother of life, and to kill the woman is equated with killing children; and killing children is killing humanity itself. Therefore, the woman should be handled with respect and not be treated as if she is a slave.

Even the woman who is advanced in age has a considerable value and blessing before men. This is what the proverb utters: "It is better to be married to an old lady than to remain unmarried." This proverb indicates that some areas of human life can be satisfied by the woman alone. The man who stays without marriage lacks an incredible thing. One Maasai proverb explains this fact when it says: "It is at five that man succeeds." The Maasai of Kenya are the ones who mostly use this proverb. For them it has something to say about a successful life of a husband. According to them, a successful husband requires "a wife, a cow, a sheep, a goat, and a donkey." This would mean that even if one is rich, he is hardly successful as long as he lacks a wife.[21]

The Tsonga and Shangana people of South Africa (Azania) say: "To beget a woman is to beget a man." This saying is not empty in itself. It carries with it a hope after marriage. Married people hope that after marriage, the wife will bear children, both girls and boys. So it is said, for example: "The woman who has children does not desert her home." This means that the woman is given security through bearing children, becomes joyful, is taken care of in her old age, and is respected by the husband and the wider society.

So the proverb which says "the woman whose sons have died is richer than a barren woman" planned to say that it is possible for the woman who bore children and lost them because of deaths to be provided an excuse over the one who does not bear due to barrenness. The blessing brought about by a parent is often associated with the proverb that goes: "May you bear children like bees! May you bear children like calabash seeds!" Today's economic and

21. Taysense, "Role of Women in Africa."

educational pressure will force a change in these sentiments where parents feel the need to reduce the number of children they can support and educate adequately.

This sentiment is aired in another proverb from the Gikuyu of Kenya, which states thus: "The baby that refuses its mother's breast will never be full." Other people may feed the baby or the person, but their food would never satisfy as well as that provided by the mother.

All the proverbs stated above and many others not stated indicate that the mother's role cannot be 100 percent duplicated. She is the provider of the unsurpassed love and immeasurable kindness, warmness, adequate care, bodily and emotional nourishment, and much more. This concern begins already when the person is inside the mother's womb and lasts (or should last) until the mother has died, or indeed, it continues when she dies and becomes a spirit, a living dead. It also means that the love, the care and tenderness, should be reciprocated by everyone towards his or her own mother because everyone has a mother. So, it is because of the mentioned roles of the mother that we hear proverbs like "A child does not laugh at the ugliness of his mother" from the Lugbara of Uganda, or "The mother of the big he-goat has no horns" from the Akamba of Kenya.

According to Mbiti, there are many beautiful things said about women. Men will fight among themselves because of women—to show the extent at which they value the women concerned. So in Ghana we hear that "Two bosom friends that vie for one and the same lady have chosen a common read to be each other's enemies." Compared to a man, the woman is more precious, as it is said: "The woman is a banana tree (which multiplies itself); the man however, is a cornstalk (which stands alone)." It is also from Ghana where we have the beautiful comparison and mutual complement between the wife and the husband: "Woman is a flower in a garden; her husband, the fence around it." So the above sayings indicate that women need all the protection which men can provide them.

Despite the positive depiction of women by the above proverbs, there are some proverbs that depict them negatively. In some proverbs, women are depicted as sexual objects, dependant creatures, vulnerable, or as inferior beings in society. We present below two examples of proverbs from the Igbo of Nigeria to illustrate this point: The first example indicates the vulnerable nature of the female body. "*Nwa-agbogho Ugwuta si nne ya na otu nwoke ka ya naagara onwe ya, o wee tuburu ya raa. Nne ya wee si ya gaa rakwuru. O gaa, a rachie ya ozo.* (An Ugwuta [Oguta] girl told her mother that as she was going on her way, a man came and threw her down and sexed [raped] her. Her mother told her to go and retaliate. She went, and was sexed [raped] again.)"[22] This proverb indicates the sexual vulnerability of women in relation to men caused by their sexual differences.

The second proverb indicates that women are dependent beings. "*Anaghi atu ikpu ukwu egwu maka na o bughi ya gaara ownwe ya.* (One cannot be afraid of the wide vagina because it cannot sex itself.)"[23] This proverb depicts the female vagina as being dependent on the male penis. It is viewed as helpless in itself. The value of the vagina is seen when sexed by the male's penis, and therefore, portrays the woman as a possession of the man. Hence, the above examples of negative proverbs indicate that women have been made inferior through the use of proverbs in some African ethnic groups, which suggest the need to reshape culture in terms of relationship between men and women. The examples indicate that the female bodies abused for so long are as valuable as those of men, and men's chauvinistic approach over bodies of women have done more harm to women's status than good.[24]

---

22. Obododimma, "Semantics of Female Devaluation," 92; Hussein, "Social and Ethno-Cultural Construction," 66.

23. Obododimma, "Semantics of Female Devaluation," 92.

24. Obododimma, "Semantics of Female Devaluation"; cf. Mmadike, "Igbo Perception of Womanhood"; Chikwelu, "Never Marry a Woman with Big Feet."

CONCLUSION

This section has portrayed missionaries' encounter with African peoples and cultures, an encounter that manifested asymmetrical power relations. These power relations were apparent in the oppressions of racism, imperialism, and sexism, whereby African women suffered triple oppression. Indeed, while African males gained access to formal education provided by the missionaries, and further to formal theological education, African women were marginalized. This was where the asymmetrical treatment of men and women was manifested, causing them demand equality in various spheres of relationships.

The sidelining of women in Africa presents us with a somewhat similar situation that led to the emergence of Western feminism; the difference is that, while Western feminism is engaged primarily with the oppression of sexism, women in Africa encounter oppression of racism and imperialism together with sexism. However, in both the contexts of African women and that which gave rise to the history of Western feminism, women have worked together for their emancipation.

We have also looked at how the importance of women is spelled out through myths and proverbs. These myths and proverbs in various African ethnic groups show the need for mutuality and complementarity between males and females. Furthermore, they show how women in a community have a role in its continuity and how they have been sidelined by those myths and proverbs. Generally, we can conclude with Kasomo, who says: "In Africa often women have been treated as 'second–class' as portrayed in many African proverbs and sayings. In most of these proverbs, women are referred to as stoves, old cooking pots, large wooden stirring spoons, hoes, cows, merino sheep, fields and fires and even dogs usually with a derogatory meaning. 'Does woman speak in public?' 'Is the woman considered person?'"[25] Despite this depiction, yet women remain as important as men with equal rights in various spheres of relationships.

25. Kasomo, "Role of Women," 128.

CHAPTER REVIEW

1. Define African Traditional Religion.

2. Explain the attitude of missionaries towards the African Traditional Religion.

3. Describe the status of women within the African Traditional Religion.

4. Discuss the way in which the African woman is depicted in African mythology and proverbs.

Chapter 5

WOMEN WITHIN CHRISTIANITY

INTRODUCTION

In this section, we look at some texts in both the Old and New Testaments which portray the role of women. We seek to see how women are depicted and how we can analyze this depiction. However, the role model of our current church is how women were depicted in the early church tradition. In the early church, women had plenty of roles which identified their significance. Some of the women we come across were disciples of Jesus, evangelists, missionaries, and financiers of the ministry by hosting fellow Christians. Here, the question is the following: Have theology and scriptural interpretations heeded to the above-stated roles of women through the life of the church?

In response to the above question, Casimir et al. have stated: "In Africa, oppressive, cultural and socio-economic practices coupled with theological misinterpretation of key religious literature such as the Bible have encouraged centuries old injustice and inequality that have denied the recognition of women's roles in development."[1] Thus, following the above-stated role of Scriptures

1. Casimir et al., "Church and Gender Equality," 170.

towards women, we examine some women in the Bible and then proceed to understanding the appearance of *The Woman's Bible*. We consider some women who appear in the Bible, and further provide a sketch of their stories as illustrated in the biblical texts. In so doing, reflections on their roles and depiction may be many. This is where we start from.

Clearly, there is scant knowledge of women in the Bible. It is limited and sketchy. To remedy this, we have feminist biblical scholars trying to delve further into this area. There are without a doubt some recurring themes in feminist biblical scholarship: the extensive influence of patriarchy in the Bible as a whole. We wish to consider women forebears, the women of the Bible, whether Israelites, Jews, or Christians, whom we find when we trace about women's history. [2]

WOMEN IN THE BIBLE

African women theologians, like Musa Dube, have shown that the Bible, gender, and African Christianity are constantly negotiated positions in different denominations, ethnicities, forms of Christianity, countries and times. Granted this variety, for our purpose, we take as an entry point the discussion by Stanton. In the introduction to *The Woman's Bible*, Stanton states:

> The canon and civil law; church and state; priests and legislators; all political parties and religious denominations have alike taught that woman was made after man, of man, and for man, an inferior being, subject to man. Creeds, codes, Scriptures and statutes, are all based on this idea. The fashions, forms, ceremonies and customs of society, church ordinances and discipline all grow out of this idea.[3]

Stanton's statement above indicates that the Bible and its tradition have held a patriarchal point of view since their inception. There

2. Cf. Togarasei, "Legacy of Circle Women's Engagement."

3. Stanton, *Woman's Bible*, 7.

are many depictions in the Bible that indicate an asymmetrical relationship between men and women which cause Christianity to be accused of humiliating women. Few examples can suffice: Paul writes: "Wives, submit to your husbands as to the Lord, for the husband is the head of the wife as Christ is the head of the church" (Eph 5: 22, 23). Peter also says: "Slaves, submit yourselves to your masters with all respect, not only to those who are good and considerate, but also to those who are harsh" (1 Pet 2:18). Then he adds: "Wives, in the same way be submissive to your husbands" (1 Pet 3:1). Therefore, as Casimir et al. state, Christianity has for centuries used the "submission" clause to oppress women without its adequate due interpretations. This misuse of the "submission" clause is what made Pope Paul II apologize to women about what the church had done for centuries, since the Inquisition.[4] In their own words, Casimir et al. state: "Pope John Paul II made a historic apology to several groups oppressed by the church since its inquisition started. The late pontiff's apology to women as a group was as a result of the obnoxious and oppressive denial of women's human right by the Church and the greater society because of the wrong interpretation of the 'submission' clause in the Bible."[5]

Nunes and Deventer further emphasize that "Bible passages like the second creation story in Genesis 2:4b—3:24, the author's (Paul?) affirmation of men's headship in 1 Timothy 2:11–14, women's speaking in church being prohibited in 1 Corinthians 14:35–35 and women being taught to obey their husbands (Eph. 5:22–24; Col. 3:18–19; 1 Pet. 3:1–6) were all interpreted in such a way that people believe women's authority must be surrendered to their husbands and so to men in general."[6] All of these texts have long been misinterpreted in favor of male domination over women for centuries. However, for the sake of this chapter, we narrow down the discussion to only two women, namely Eve and Mary Magdalene, located in the Old and New Testaments respectively.

---

4. Casimir et al., "Church and Gender Equality," 166.

5. Casimir et al., "Church and Gender Equality," 166.

6. Nunes and Deventer, "Feminist Interpretation," 739.

Eve—The First Woman

The First Creation Account in Genesis 1:26–28 reads:

> Then God said, "Let us make man in our image, after
> our likeness. And let them have dominion over the fish
> of the sea and over the birds of the heavens and over the
> livestock and over all the earth and over every creeping
> thing that creeps on the earth." So God created man in
> his own image, in the image of God he created him; male
> and female he created them. And God blessed them. And
> God said to them, "Be fruitful and multiply and fill the
> earth and subdue it and have dominion over the fish of
> the sea and over the birds of the heavens and over every
> living thing that moves on the earth."

In Genesis 3:20, the man called his wife's name Eve because she
was the mother of all the living. We are told that she was named by
Adam. Clifford summarizes her depiction: "She is the first woman,
made by God from the rib of the first man. She listed to a serpent,
yielded to temptation, and compounded her sin by tempting her
husband. The wages of Eve's and Adam's sin is death."[7] According
to Phyllis Trible, most interpreters have used the interpretation of
Genesis 2–3, the second creation account and especially Genesis
2:21–24, to assert male dominance and female weakness as being
God's determination. This dominant use of texts is usually the
familiar reason for the subordination of women. However, Trible
depicts the equality between Eve and Adam based on their origi-
nator. Both Eve and Adam are works of the divine. Adam has no
part in the creation of Eve. God made him fall into a deep sleep
and took the rib of Adam. God also created Adam from mud. This
scene indicates that both of them were created from mud in a different way, according to materials which God willed to use—the
rib used to create Eve comes from mud, and the mud used to create Adam is mud. Therefore, mud is the original source of creation
of both of them.[8]

7. Clifford, *Introducing Feminist Theology*, 66.
8. Trible, "Eve and Adam."

Though the precise date of the composition of Genesis 2–3 can hardly be determined accurately, biblical scholars nevertheless argue that, due to the different narrative motifs, it certainly took an extended period for its complete formation. The main narrative was probably written down in the time of the monarchy. However, how several of the motifs are connected is still not clear.

The Genesis account is a story of creation, and at the same time an explanatory myth or etiology which was intended to explain why people get married and have pain at childbirth, why serpents lack legs, etc. It should be considered that all peoples of the world have myths that explain their origins. Similarly, the Genesis account is a myth based on the forefathers of the Jews. Hence, knowing the probable historical context in which this text was created and the type of literature it represents still hardly helps remedy the many faulty interpretations of Genesis that have been used to oppress women for centuries.

In the midst of the rampant use of the text, we can have questions that raise our suspicion. Some of these questions are the following: What then can we say about Eve? What can we say about her conversation with the serpent? Why was Eve more assertive, independent, a thinker, and a communicator? Where was Adam at that time? Why was the stone silent? Can we say that if Adam had any contribution, he would have spoken? Or, perhaps, he had forgotten everything he was told by God? All these questions are possible in a feminist hermeneutics of suspicion.

A feminist hermeneutics of suspicion is an activity focusing on raising consciousness to people which require those people to take into account the influence of culturally determined gender roles and attitudes on the Bible. It includes a systematic analysis seeking to uncover its causes in biblical society, church, and the academy. It focuses on exploring oppressive and liberating values and visions inscribed in the text. It does the exploration by identifying the androcentric patriarchal characters and dynamics of the text. In so doing, it seeks to investigate how and why the text constructs certain stories whose central texts are women in the way it does.

By way of a hermeneutics of suspicion, it is no longer acceptable simply to take the traditional interpretations of the text, nor the texts themselves, as indicative of the original event.[9] It is quite obvious that all sorts of power-dynamics were at play in the formation of our Christian tradition. This being known, feminists have helped to design critical tools to excavate beneath the present interpretations and unearth the original revelation. Its first assumption is that patriarchy affects biblical texts and their interpretations in the Christian tradition. Therefore, biblical texts should be examined for their possible androcentric assumptions and positions.

Androcentricism refers to male-centeredness, which is the value set by our dominant culture based on male norms. This concept was used by Charlotte Perkins Gilman to draw attention to male bias in relating to the opposite sex. In sum, any account which characterizes aspects of women's lives as deviant is androcentric. We look at how biblical texts treat women in stories and laws; and how biblical texts neglect women experiences completely. Therefore, feminist theologians have offered the church altogether new insights into the nature of God, God's way with us, and a commitment to a distinctive way of doing theology.

On the other hand stands the hermeneutic of remembrance. This hermeneutic recovers the sufferings which women suffered in the past and of all persons subjugated through enslavement, exile, and persecution. It serves as a "dangerous memory" since it is often subversive. In the midst of crisis, biblical figures of the distant past found in their relationship with God hope to go on and hope for the possibility of becoming agents of liberation. It reclaims the struggles of women of past decades and attempts to reconstruct their history. It is conscious that the canonical Scriptures relate only part of the experience of the early church. In that way, it seeks to develop a feminist critical method and historical model for moving beyond the androcentric text to the history of women in biblical religion.

Trible shows several things in the reinterpretation of the creation narrative. According to her, created simultaneously from the

9. Schussler-Fiorenza, *Rhetoric and Ethics*, 36–37.

earth creature (*ha adam*), male (*ish*) and female (*ishah*) are not superior and subordinate to each other. Neither one has power over the other; in fact, both are given equal power because they both come from the unfinished earth creature, which was originally created from the earth (*ha adama*). Though the parallelism within the poem alone suggests this latter point, the context substantiates it. As we have seen in the verse immediately preceding, God proposes, by using a plural verb form, that *adam* (earth creature) be given dominion over all the earth: "let *them* have dominion" (1:26). Moreover, the man confirms by saying the woman is "bone of my bones and flesh of my flesh" (2: 23), which implies unity, solidarity, equality, and mutuality of man and woman. As they both originate from the unfinished earth creature, they are given equal power to have dominion over other creatures, with not one to have dominion over the other. This equal power was probably what God intended for the two created human beings. Moreover, in the verses that follow, God blesses male and female, using the plural "them," consistently speaking "to them" with plural verb forms (1:28–29).[10]

We focus on the interpretation of the meaning of the term "companion" as Trible views it. According to Trible, "companion" is the preferred translation of the Hebrew word *ezer*; yet in English, it is often translated as "helper." This word "helper" suggests an assistant, which leads to raising an argument that women were created to assist men, and therefore are subordinates to the men they assist. Yet, the Old Testament uses the same word, *ezer*, to depict God as being the helper of Israel. Certainly, this usage does not imply that God is subordinate to humans. Since the same word has been used to indicate God being a helper of humans, it most likely means that *ezer* is a relational term designating a beneficial relationship without a hint of subordination. Hence, Trible's translation of *ezer* as companion denotes that woman is a

---

10. Trible, "Eve and Adam"; cf. Clifford, *Introducing Feminist Theology*, 68–70.

true counterpart to the man, corresponding in every way to him as another fully human creature of God.[11]

By contrast, Kostenberger and Jones see no such implication. To them, Genesis 2 does not teach that she may merely act as the man's "helper" when she so chooses; but rather, that serving as the man's "helper" sums up her very reason for existence in relation to the man.[12] Moreover, Stanton, in her critical appraisal of the creation narrative, states: "woman was made after man, of man and for man, an inferior being, subject to man."[13]

In Genesis, Eve is mentioned *by name* only once more when she is said to bear two sons, Cain and Abel. Further, we see that there is an androcentric pattern that follows in her story, especially in the genealogies that follow as recorded in Genesis 4:17–26.[14] Therefore, we conclude this discussion about Eve by an extensive quotation from Casimir *et al.* Quoting from Uchem, Casimir *et al.* write:

> A literal mindset, opposed to the symbolical and mytho-logical consciousness characteristic of the milieu in which it arose, was imposed on the story. Over time, the symbol of the rib, meant to convey a sense of oneness be-came a tool of oppression. The symbol of the rib is taken to denote weakness, inferiority and a secondary place in creation. However, those who advanced these views fail to reason that the woman who was supposedly made from "human stuff" (the rib) the might be superior to the man who was supposedly made from "dust." Moreover, those who argue that man is pre-eminent because he was created before the woman need to remember that wild beasts were created before the man and would therefore be considered superior to the man. Regardless that God is our "helper" par excellence, the biblical notion of woman as "helper" has, for many years, been understood as an

11. See Trible, "Eve and Adam"; cf. Clifford, *Introducing Feminist Theology,* 68.

12. See Kostenberger and Jones, *God, Marriage, and Family,* 26.

13. Stanton, *Woman's Bible,* 7

14. Clifford, *Introducing Feminist Theology,* 71.

indication of her lesser status in relation to the man. In my view, this has been at the root of gender inequality in the Church and has reinforced myths of male superiority, and female inferiority and functionality in the different cultures of the world. *This is evident in the numerous anti-women sentiments and teachings of many Fathers of the Church.* As long as this notion of "helper" remains in force, it will continue to undermine the realization of gender equality in the church and in the society.[15]

It should be clear that the purpose of God to create the woman was not identifying the status of the two people, the male and the female (at the pre-fall); most likely God's purpose centered on the two creatures supporting each other in their task of sustaining the rest of creation. At the post-fall the woman was punished by God to be under the man's dominion. This dominion is cemented by the tenth commandment given to Israel, which lists a woman among the man's properties: slaves, wife, cattle, etc. (Exod 20:17; Deut 5:21). However, looking in front to the fulfillment of the Old Testament, the original sin of Eve and its punishments have been broken by Jesus and his death and resurrection in the New Testament.

Despite the above possible interpretation of the creation narrative basing on the pre-fall, the post-fall, and Jesus' restoration of the dignity of humanity (male and female), women have been mistreated throughout the life of the church due to scriptural misinterpretations.

Kasomo, taking a statement from the Vatican Council II, reiterates:

> It is the unbroken tradition of the Catholic Church that women have never been admitted to the holy orders, with which the orthodox tradition also concurs. Jesus Christ did not call any woman to be part of the twelve, even his own mother. The apostolic church faithfully carried out this exclusion of women from priesthood that was instituted by Christ. Moreover, it should also be said that the maleness of the priest reflects the sacramental mystery

15. Casimir *et al.,* "Church and Gender Equality," 70–71 (italics added).

of Christ and the church. As a representative of the head of the church the bridegroom, the priest must be male. There must be "natural resemblance" between the priest and Christ. For Christ himself was and remains a male (Vatican declaration, 1976).[16]

This position opens a room for more critical comment and discussion and shall not be provided herein. To conclude this section, we can say that the first woman has been held responsible for the emergence of sin in the world. This notion has been stated by Stanton in her introduction to *The Woman's Bible*: "The Bible teaches that woman brought sin and death into the world, that she precipitated the fall of the race, that she was arraigned before the judgement seat of Heaven, tried, condemned, and sentenced. Marriage for her was to be a condition of bondage, maternity a period of suffering and anguish, and in silence and subjection, she was to play the role of a dependant on man's bounty for all her material wants, and for all the information she might desire on the vital questions of the hour, she was commanded to ask her husband at home."[17]

Mary Magdalene–The Traditionally Misconceived Woman

We now turn our discussion to the second woman: Mary Magdalene.[18] Mary Magdalene is mentioned in all four Gospels (Matt 27:55–56; Mark 15:40–41; Luke 8:2–3) as being one of the important women in Galilee who followed and supported Jesus. The text depicts Mary Magdalene as the one who was liberated from the shackles of the seven demons (Luke 8:2; cf. Mark 16:9) and as the one who sat at the foot of the cross of Jesus with Mary the mother of Jesus and Mary Clopas (John 19:25). She is the witness of the

16. Kasomo, "Role of Women," 127–28.

17. Stanton, *Woman's Bible*, 7.

18. The name "Magdalene" "is usually regarded as referring to Mary's hometown of Magdala, a fishing center on the Sea of Galilee (although it should be noted that there is no first-century reference to a town by that name)" (Beavis, "Who is Mary Magdalene?," 23–24).

burial of Jesus together with other women (Mark 15:47; Matt 27:60–61; Luke 23:50—24:10). In the text from the Gospel according to Matthew, Mary Magdalene together with another Mary are the first to see the risen Jesus (28:1–10). In Mark's tradition, she is the first to see the risen Jesus (Mark 16:9). In John, she comes alone to the tomb and is the first to receive the instructions to go to tell the other disciples the good news of his resurrection (John 20:1–18). Therefore, the textual depiction of Mary Magdalene is positive, considering her a woman of value to society as the "apostle of the apostles" since the time of medieval theologians.

The stereotyped image of Mary Magdalene is found in the Western European rendering of Luke 7:36–50. We recapitulate the text here as recorded in *The New King James Version*:

Then one of the Pharisees asked Him to eat with him. And He went to the Pharisee's house, and sat down to eat. And behold, a woman in the city who was a sinner, when she knew that *Jesus* sat at the table in the Pharisee's house, brought an alabaster flask of fragrant oil, and stood at His feet behind *Him* weeping; and she began to wash His feet with her tears, and wiped *them* with the hair of her head; and she kissed His feet and anointed *them* with the fragrant oil. Now when the Pharisee who had invited Him saw *this,* he spoke to himself, saying, "This Man, if He were a prophet, would know who and what manner of woman *this is* who is touching Him, for she is a sinner." And Jesus answered and said to him, "Simon, I have something to say to you." So he said, "Teacher, say it." "There was a certain creditor who had two debtors. One owed five hundred denarii, and the other fifty. And when they had nothing with which to repay, he freely forgave them both. Tell Me, therefore, which of them will love him more?" Simon answered and said, "I suppose the *one* whom he forgave more." And He said to him, "You have rightly judged." Then He turned to the woman and said to Simon, "Do you see this woman? I entered your house; you gave Me no water for My feet, but she has washed My feet with her tears and wiped *them* with the hair of her head. You gave Me no kiss, but this woman has not ceased to kiss My feet since the time I came in. You did not anoint My head with oil, but this woman has anointed My feet with fragrant oil. Therefore, I say to you, her sins, which *are* many, are forgiven, for she loved much. But to whom little is forgiven, *the same* loves little." Then He said to her, "Your sins are forgiven." And those who sat at the table with Him began to say to themselves, "Who is this who even forgives sins?" Then He said to the woman, "Your faith has saved you. Go in peace."

Clifford asserts that

Mary Magdalene, due to patriarchal misinterpretations of Luke 7:36–50 and 8:2, has often been identified as the repentant prostitute who redirected to Jesus the 'love' that she formerly distributed for her sexual favors to her paying customers. This interpretation has a long history in Christianity, traceable to the time of Pope Gregory the Great (ca. 540—604 C.E.)[19]

who, in about 591 CE, authoritatively pronounced that Mary the repentant sinner of Luke's Gospel and Mary Magdalene were one. However, scholars have shown that there is a "lack of logic in the depiction of Mary as a prostitute, the prototype of a sinful woman and the New Testament's counterpart to the sinful Eve."[20] The question is this: Why does the offence have to do with sex? By the way, the woman who anointed Jesus in Luke 7 does not bear any name; this unnaming most likely indicates that she was not Mary Magdalene, who had her own standing in society. Had she been the one, she would have been named, since by then she had already become well-known among the early Christians.[21] Therefore, confusion has occurred between the woman in Luke 7:36–50 who was unnamed, self-invited at the dinner, considered to be a sinner, and went to Jesus anointing his feet, and another Mary who was the

19. Clifford, *Introducing Feminist Theology*, 78.
20. Clifford, *Introducing Feminist Theology*, 78.
21. Clifford, *Introducing Feminist Theology*, 78.

sister of Martha and Lazarus of Bethany and anointed Jesus at their home (John 12:1–8).

What is the difference between the two women? The difference between them lies on how one describes their character. The woman in Luke is a sinner and appears as a self-invited person at the house of the Pharisee. The major point of focus in this story is the woman and her act of repentance and the forgiveness of her sins. This depiction is different from the Mary in John's Gospel, who appears as a friend of Jesus (see John 11:5), and the one who anoints Jesus in gratitude for Jesus' mighty deed of raising Lazarus; the anointing act is done at her brother's home (see John 12:1). These two women cannot be the same; and Mary Magdalene cannot be identified with either of them.

Moreover, to connect the release of Mary Magdalene from the seven demons with immoral behavior or prostitution, as has been done by Western scholars for many centuries, is implausible. She might have been suffering from epilepsy or another mental disease.[22] Mary Magdalene, the woman sent to proclaim the good news of Jesus' resurrection to his followers, is more appropriately remembered as the "apostle to the apostles" rather than a repentant prostitute, as depicted by the counterfeit or skewed interpretations of the Western European traditions. Therefore, this latter notion of Mary Magdalene as a repentant sinner (a prostitute) is more likely of a patriarchal projection of male imagination that has ever dominated the Western European art and literature.[23]

THE WOMAN'S BIBLE

After discussing the two women and their depiction in the biblical scholarship, we now turn to *The Woman's Bible*. In 1995, it was 100 years since *The Woman's Bible* appeared in New York, the first volume of a work that created both a sensation and indignation. Some greeted it as the work of Satan, while others viewed it as

22. Clifford, *Introducing Feminist Theology*, 78.

23. Harmer, "One Woman with Many Faces"; cf. Clifford, *Introducing Feminist Theology*, 78.

a piece of sectarianism harmful to the efforts of emancipation. Others feared to jeopardize their evangelical reputation, especially those who believed the Bible to be "the word of God," not to be compromised. For others still, it was received as an appropriate expression of their suffering at the hands of the structures of women's oppression found in churches, congregations, and state politics.[24]

Elizabeth Cady Stanton, already in her seventies, was credited with coming up with *The Woman's Bible*. It had been her life's work to struggle against discrimination enshrined in the law. Together with her spouse, a lawyer by profession, she toiled as an abolitionist. Already in the late 1830s she came to know women who, unlike herself, fought against discrimination in the religious circles.[25] One such women was Sarah Grimké, who already saw the connection between the liberation of slaves and that of women, not least because the Bible-believing men often prevented them from addressing an audience publicly. In 1837, Sarah Grimké proposed that the interpretation of Scripture by men serves the suppression of women. She therefore encouraged women to take up the study of the languages of the sacred texts so that they could take up interpretation for themselves.

Angeline and Sarah Grimké were born in Charleston, South Carolina in the United States. Sarah was born on November 26, 1792, and Angeline was born on February 20, 1802. Their father, John, was the then-Judge of the Supreme Court of South Carolina. The two Grimké sisters grew under the strict adherence of discipline exerted by their father and their mother, Mary. These two sisters, based on the strict life they lived, became prominent women's

24 Cf. Stanton, *Woman's Bible*, 9.

25 Lochhead writes that "During the 1840s, women maintained their abolition work despite the tremendous resistance fuelled by racism, sexism, and conservative religious ideology. By the end of the decade, many women agreed on the need for a women's rights movement. Denied participation at the World's Anti-Slavery Convention in London 1840 because of their gender, Lucretia Mott and Elizabeth Cady Stanton decided to organize a women's rights convention. A group of women, many of them abolitionists, set this new movement in motion in July 1848 in Seneca Falls, New York" (Lochhead, "Turning the World Upside Down," 10; cf. Lerner, *Feminist Thought of Sarah Grimké*").

rights advocates and antislavery leaders in the United States in the nineteenth century. They were the first women to provide a clear distinction between sex and gender and to write a biblical argument in favour of women's equality with men.[26] Sarah, Angeline, and Stanton all attended an international congress of abolitionists in 1840, and this was a key event for them because it brought together the struggle for the liberation of slaves and that of women. Stanton had begun to toil in her own context for the equality of women, being recognized as one of the mothers of the gathering held between July 19–20, 1848, at the Wesleyan Methodist Church in Seneca Falls, a gathering that has become part of the history of women's liberation. The convention agreed on several things that ignited the North American movement of women:

1. The vote for women

2. Women's education

3. Legal independence from their fathers and husbands

It was the debate on the existing laws that brought home to Elizabeth Cady Stanton the way in which the Bible was drawn on as divine authority for the religious as well as political legitimating of the injustice vested on women in the guise of law. Her contention was the contradiction of human rights that many people of faith were holding onto.

Such enlightenment thinking, which had shaped her whole life, stirred her upon the death of her husband to initiate her project, *The Woman's Bible*, and to see its successful conclusion. She died at the age of eighty-eight in 1902. The women with whom Stanton worked had no intention of interfering with the theologians' scholarly pursuits. Their aims were far more basic: to unmask, with the help of educated reason of women, the church's and the state's misuse of the Bible—or more precisely, to unmask the

---

26. For their early life, their entrance into the slavery abolition movement and their activities in the abolition movement see Lewis, "Angeline Grimké Weld," 21–77; and Lerner, *Feminist Thought of Sarah Grimké*.

inclination of misusing the Bible that was rooted in its very own deficiencies while thereby undermining its divine authority.

The general outlay of *The Woman's Bible* as a piece follows the order of the biblical writings. Yet they are not commented on sequentially. The texts are assessed through summaries which retell events. In other sections, there are studies of selected sections and passages which were often used in the United States to legitimize the inequality of women before the law. She did not compose the entire text; rather, she composed the base text and then called for contributions from other women, which she then put together. In accomplishing this task, she gathered about a dozen women who were versed in literature, history, and Greek.[27]

The main issue for Stanton was to advance public discussion of the equality of women. Let us consider the parable of the ten virgins' piece of work from *The Woman's Bible*. We recapitulate the text thus as it appears there (numbers of verses removed):

> *Matthew xxv.1–12* Then shall the kingdom of heaven be likened unto ten virgins, which took their lamps, and went forth to meet the bridegroom. And five of them were wise, and five were foolish. They that were foolish took their lamps, and took no oil with them: But the wise took oil in their vessels with their lamps. While the bridegroom tarried, they all slumbered and slept. And at midnight there was a cry made, Behold, the bridegroom cometh; go ye out to meet him. Then all those virgins arose, and trimmed their lamps. And the foolish said unto the wise, Give us of your oil; for our lamps are gone out. But the wise answered, saying, Not so, lest there be not enough for us and you: but go ye rather to them that sell, and buy for yourselves. And while they went to buy, the bridegroom came; and they that were ready went in with him to the marriage: and the door was shut. Afterward came also the other virgins, saying, Lord, Lord, open to us. But he answered and said, Verily I say unto you, I know you not.

27. See Stanton, *Woman's Bible*, 9.

The central issue in the above text, according to Stanton, is "the duty of self-development, repeatedly urged in the form of parables" being stated directing to both women and men.[28] Stanton considers one's negligence of his or her talents and abilities to do things, trying to bury them down, to be sinful. She continues to note that Adam Clarke, in his commentaries, explains this parable as one that refers mainly to spiritual gifts and religious life. He provides interesting depictions of the aspects of the parable: the Lord of Hosts is portrayed as being the bridegroom; the judgment day is portrayed as being the wedding feast; and the foolish virgins are portrayed as being the sinners whose hearts "were cold and dead being devoid of all spiritual graces and as being unfit to enter the kingdom of heaven." To Clarke, the wise virgins were the saints ready for the bridal procession in celebration of the wedding feast. Hence, as depicted in the parable, the celebrations of these weddings were done mostly during the night and were expected to begin when the evening star rose. Moreover, his parable depicts that there was a delay from the normal beginning time of the feast.[29]

However, Stanton contends that this parable seems to apply more to this life than to that which is to come; it applies to the intellectual and the moral nature. Furthermore, it fairly describes the two classes of people in society: a class of those who have never learned the important duty of cultivating their individual powers to use the talents given to them to keep the lamps timmed and burning, being likened as the foolish virgins; and a class of those who have have learned that important duty, likened as wise virgins. To Stanton, the idea of being a helpmate to somebody else has been drilled into many women that an individual life, aim, and purpose are never taken into consideration. Therefore, to her, this simple parable teaches us to cultivate courage and self-reliance. The virgins in this parable are summoned to an important duty at midnight, alone, in darkness, and in solitude. No gentleman is there to run for oil and trim their lamps. They must depend on themselves, unsupported. Perhaps the foolish virgins had wasted many precious hours

28. Stanton, *Woman's Bible*, 126.
29. Clarke, *New Testament of Our Lord*, 218.

on their male relatives, when they should have been trimming their own lamps and keeping oil in their vessels.

Now, to Stanton, there is nothing admirable in the action of young women begging for funds to educate young men while they are too poor to educate themselves; and if able, they are still deprived of access into institutions of learning. Woman's dedication to the comfort, the education, and the success of men in general, is due to her self-sacrifice having been so long and so sweetly lauded by poets, philosophers, and priests. Indeed, it is not laudable for women to put together donation parties for churches in which they are not given the chance to pray, preach, or share in the offices and honors.[30]

Stanton laments that in their lack of knowledge, women endeavor to provide education to the men within their family unit, and in doing that they make "themselves ladders by which their husbands, brothers, and sons climb up into the kingdom of knowledge, while they themselves are shut out from all intellectual companionship . . . [and] have not kept their own lamps trimmed and burning, no oil in their vessels, and no reserve in themselves."[31] These are likened with the foolish virgins who stayed unprepared until the coming of the bride.

STANTON'S INTERPRETATION

The wise virgins keep their lamps orderly, with burning oil in their vessels for their own use. They go further, taking advantage of every opportunity for their education so as to secure a healthy and complete development. They also enter all the profitable avenues of labor for self-support, so that when opportunities and responsibilities of life come, they enjoy having advanced themselves.[32]

Advancing the above assertion, Stanton states,

---

30. Stanton, *Woman's Bible*, 126.
31. Stanton, *Woman's Bible*, 126.
32. Stanton, *Woman's Bible*, 127.

These are the women who to-day are close upon the heels of man in the whole realm of thought, in art, in science, in literature and in government. With telescopic vision they explore the starry firmament, and bring back the history of the planetary world. With chart and compass they pilot ships across the mighty deep, and with skilful fingers send electric messages around the world. In galleries of art, the grandeur of nature and the greatness of humanity are immortalized by them on canvas, and by their inspired touch, dull blocks of marble are transformed into angels of light. In music they speak again the language of Mendelssohn, of Beethoven, of Chopin, of Schumann, and are worthy interpreters of their great souls. The poetry and the novels of the century are theirs; they, too, have touched the keynote of reform in religion, in politics and in social life. They fill the editors' and the professors' chairs, plead at the bar of justice, walk the wards of the hospital, and speak from the pulpit and the platform. Such is the widespread preparation for the marriage feast of science and religion; such is the type of womanhood which the bridegroom of an enlightened public sentiment welcomes to-day; and such is the triumph of the wise virgins over the folly, the ignorance and the degradation of the past as in grand procession they enter the temple of knowledge, and the door is no longer shut.[33]

Therefore, for Stanton, in putting together a Bible for women, we are availed to something more like a commentary on Scripture from the perspectives of feminism. Stanton places her subjective judgment upon each passage. This avails us a different lens from which to read biblical texts. This is not to say that this interpretation is the only valid one, but that this is one plausible way of reading the parable of the ten virgins.

33. Stanton, *Woman's Bible*, 127.

CONCLUSION

This chapter has surveyed some evidence to show the status of women as depicted in the Christian textual tradition. Clearly, the Christian textual tradition has a lot to say on women in religion. The textual tradition has been noted as not being neutral in itself. Rather, it espouses androcentric and patriarchal frames which have an impact on the reader. The Bible has depicted women as being inferior beings subject to the authority of men. Reinterpretations of certain texts have been suggested, especially the creation narrative and the text of the repentant sinner in the Gospel of John, with the latter focusing on the parable of the ten virgins. It is likely that several years after *The Woman's Bible* was written, a commentary on the same parable begins by positing that the use of the term "virgins" sharply negates the sexuality of the personalities in the narrative, and as such should not be celebrated. Hence, with the example texts discussed, a hermeneutic of suspicion of various androcentric biblical texts can demonstrate that the depiction of women as inferior beings is implausible.

CHAPTER REVIEW

1. Christianity and the Bible are weapons often used to perpetuate patriarchy and male domination. Discuss this statement with concrete examples.

2. In the beginning of life, Adam and Eve were made equal, according to Genesis 3:20. State the effects of the interpretations of creation stories to the relationship between men and women.

3. What is androcentrism? How is this notion visible in the Christian Scriptures and in contemporary churches?

4. Discuss the way in which the figure of Mary Magdalene has been misconceived in Western interpretations.

5. Explain *The Woman's Bible* and the legacy of Elizabeth Cady Stanton and other abolitionists.

Chapter 6

WOMEN WITHIN ISLAM

INTRODUCTION

IN ORDER TO UNDERSTAND the situation of women in Islam, one needs to understand the situation in the pre-Islamic era, the so-called *Jahiliyyah* period—the period of ignorance and barbarism. The words of Ja'far ibn Abu Talib, who stood before the king of Abbysinia, a safe Christian kingdom, seeking asylum for himself and his group of Muslims who fled from Mecca due to persecutions of the pre-Islamic Arabia, are quoted by Sulaimani as: "O king . . . we were a people of jahiliyyah, worshipping idols, eating the raw flesh of dead animals, commiting abominations, neglecting our relatives, doing evil to our neighbours, and the strong among us would oppress the weak."[1] The stament of Abu Talib before the king of Abbyssinia indicates that in the pre-Islamic era, women faced the "culturally approved discrimination, dehumanization and social deprivation" exerted by the existing paganism.[2]

Moreover, Booley explains the status of women in this era thus:

1. Sulaimani, "Changing Position of Women," 5.
2. Okon, "Status of Woman," 21; cf. Qur'an 3:154.

The period before the introduction of Islam is generally referred to as the jahiliya period, characterised by ignorance and barbarism. During this period women were treated as an "object of sale," which led to them being exploited by their own fathers and, subsequently, by their husbands. Women were forced to accept the primary role of being wife and mother which was a product of a patriarchal society. The father possessed the right to sell his daughter in marriage to the highest bidder. The husband, in turn, exploited the wife by possessing the right to terminate the marriage at any time and for any reason.[3]

Therefore, as Sulaimani writes, "the woman in the pre-Islamic society was treated most of the time, as if she were an article of mecharndise to be sold."[4]

In this era of *Jahiliyyah*, families were in need of male children to defend them in various affairs of their lives. Okon explains briefly about the situation:

The *Jahiliyya* Arabs had a custom of burying their female children alive. It was an acceptable cultural practice for women to dance nude around the vicinity of Kaaba during the annual festival. One of the forms of marriage in pre-Islamic Arabia was by capture, women were captured and married by force without any resort to parental consent. It was Prophet Muhammad's social reforms that stopped such obnoxious criminal practices . . . Islam has done much to enhance the status of women more than any other world religion.[5]

Furthermore, Naseef adds thus in regard to the fate of the female child at its birth or after:

If the female child was fortunate enough not to be buried alive, she spent the rest of her life being oppressed and persecuted. Neglected by her parents and abused by her husband, nobody came forward to champion her cause.

3. Booley, "Divorce and the Law of *Khul*," 40.

4. Sulaimani, "Changing Position of Women," 13.

5. Booley, "Divorce and the Law of *Khul*," 40.

She was denied most human rights. She had no right to inheritance; indeed she herself was inherited like any other object and piece of furniture.[6]

Moreover, the Qur'an states thus in regard to what was going on in the pagan Arabian Peninsula: "And when the news of [the birth of] a female [child] is brought to any of them, his face becomes dark, and he is filled with inward grief! He hides himself from the people because of the evil of that which he has been informed. Shall he keep her with dishonour or bury her in the earth? Certainly, evil is their decision" (Surah 6:57–59). This text indicates the fate which the female child awaited after birth and the state of her parents. Therefore, following this background of the pre-Islamic Arabian Peninsula, to attempt to talk about women in Islam is a venture into an area which more often than not tends to overgeneralizations, and at times oversimplification.

Currently, there are close to a half a billion Muslim women inhabiting all major cities of the world. Therefore, it follows that to try and say something which holds true to all of them is virtually impossible. However, we approach this inquiry in various ways. This chapter argues that despite the various steps taken by Islam in order to reform the subjugating and discriminating aspects of the *Jahiliyyah* period in the Arabian Peninsula, there are yet traces of women subjugation in Islam portrayed in the Qur'an and the Islamic tradition, which in turn is still visible in the Muslim societies of the twenty-first century.

Islam arose in the Arabian Peninsula in the early seventh century. The religion was founded by the Prophet Muhammad, who grew up in Makah, a place where there were many cults and idols. After much struggle, he succeeded in establishing the principle of worship of one God, known as *Allah* in Arabic. Currently, Islam is reputed to be one of the fastest growing religions in the world due to its teachings, which hold Muslims together.

Muslims are held together by basic beliefs such as the belief in a continuous line of prophets culminating in the last Prophet

6. Naseef, *Women in Islam*, 33.

Muhammad, belief in the Day of Judgment, and in the text of the Qur'an. The Qur'an is said to be the literal word of God as sent down to God's prophet by *Tanzil* through the angel Gabriel.

The daily lives of Muslims living in different parts of the world are naturally very different. Therefore, their Islam is outwardly expressed in different ways. When investigating women in Islam, there are various entry points that may be deemed fruitful. These include elements directly related to the religion of Islam itself, as follows:

1. Past and present legal realities

2. Women in the Qur'an

3. Women in the Islamic tradition

4. Variety of Islamic rites in which women have traditionally participated

5. Roles permitted and enforced as a result of Muslim images of women

6. Education, political rights, and professional employment

LEGAL REALITIES IN ISLAM

In looking at the Muslim family law, the Qur'an is still considered and has always been considered to be the foundation of existing family law. The Qur'an, as a holy book of Islam, is seen as being the last in the series of divine revelations from God given in the seventh century, with the Prophet Muhammad as God's vehicle. Therefore, the changes in Muslim family law have been very slow to the fact that the regulations formulated by the Qur'an in regard to women have been adhered to very strictly.

In pre-Islamic Arabia there existed varied circumstances which are subject to myriad interpretations in our current time. There were certain women—priestesses, soothsayers, queens—who played a considerable role in society. On the other hand, it is argued that the Qur'an introduced some important changes that were of great advantage for women. Hence, present-day Muslims point out that Islam brought legal advantages for women which are little-known in most areas of the Western Christian world.

In turning to the Qur'an's injunctions for women, we find that they are clustered around major issues of the religion such as marriage and related topics, divorce, inheritance, and ownership of property and veiling and seclusion (*purdah*).[7] Primarily, Islamic law (*sharia*) is based on the Qur'an, and secondarily on those things that the prophet is supposed to have said and done called the Hadith, and to a lesser extent on analogy and legal reasoning.

The four major schools of law in the Sunni tradition (which makes up 85 percent of the Muslim population) are in general agreement on most of the aspects of the law and differ only on relatively minor points in personal and family law. According to the Qur'an, a man may marry up to four wives so long as he is able to provide for each equally. He may marry Muslim women, or a member of the Jewish faith, or a member of the Christian faith, or a slave woman. But a Muslim woman may marry only one husband, and he must be a Muslim.

Contemporary Muslim apologists are quick to point out that these restrictions are for the benefit of women ensuring that they will not be left unprotected. In Islam, marriage is not a sacrament but a legal contract; and according to the Qur'an, a woman has clearly defined legal rights in negotiating this contract. She can dictate the terms and can receive the dowry herself. She is permitted to keep this dowry (*mahr*) and maintain it as a source of personal pride and comfort.

Polygamy, the plurality of wives, is practiced variously is different places of the Muslim world. It is rare to find a man with more than two wives. In Iraq and Syria, the husband needs to secure permission from the court in order to get married to another wife other than the first wife. In Egypt, the first wife must give

7. Papanek defines the concept of *purdah*: "Purdah, meaning curtain, is the word most commonly used for the system of secluding women and enforcing high standards of female modesty. . . . The crucial characteristic of the purdah system is its limitation on interaction between women and males outside well-defined categories" (Papanek, "Purdah: Separate Worlds," 289).

permission to her husband to seek another wife other than her. In Morocco and Lebanon, the wife can stipulate in the marriage contract that she will not allow her husband to get married to another wife. These variances across regions are noteworthy as they speak to the changeability and the ongoing negotiating between law and practice. In general, the changing economic conditions have in part dictated that a man may only afford to have one wife.

Traditionally, Muslim women are married off when still young, sometimes before reaching puberty. This practice relates to the historical fact that fathers and other male relatives have been selecting grooms for women regardless of the Qur'an's guarantee that marriage should be a contract into which both the boy and the girl enter equally and willingly. While it is true that a girl cannot be forced into marriage, pressures from family and the youth of the bride have often made this prerogative difficult to exercise.

Another important issue in Islam is that of *Talaq*. Smith writes thus in regard to this issue:

> *Talaq*, divorce taken at the initiative of the man, is the most frequent form of separation. One kind of *talaq* is fully acceptable under the law, it can either be a single repudiation after the waiting period of three months to ensure that the wife is not pregnant, or three successive repudiations in three months. The triple repudiation which is the utterance of the *talaq* three times in succession without the three-month waiting period, is technically legal though so undesirable."[8]

Therefore, any form of divorce which the man initiates will be considered legitimate and legal for separation between the wife and the husband.

Divorce initiated by the wife is called *khul'*. This kind of divorce, though technically possible, has been effected nearly as often as the *talaq*. Unlike *talaq*, *khul'* cannot be executed whatever the cause; rather, a special stipulation is required in the marriage contract or should be made based on specific evidence such as the woman being deserted or being physically abused, insanity or

8. Smith, "Islam," 238.

impotence on any side, and the like. In general, Muslim apologists contend that divorce is not nearly as common in Islamic states as it is in the United States of America.

THE QUR'AN AND WOMEN

Twin themes that run throughout the chapters of the Qur'an are the realities of the oneness of God and the inevitability of the Day of Judgment. Strictly speaking, in the eyes of God both men and women are equal because both are religiously responsible for their religious duties and are fully accountable on the day of the final resurrection and judgment.

The equality between men and women is stressed by the Qur'an in some of its creation surahs. Surahs 4:1 and 7:189 say:

> He created man and woman from a single soul [person].
> And made his mate of like nature in order that He might dwell with her [in love].

And Surah 9:71 says

> that men and woman are "protecting friends" to each other, To enjoin what is just and forbid what is evil. He created for you mates from among yourself, that you might find rest and joy in them.

According to these surahs, there is no differentiation in status between men and women.

Moreover, the Qur'an makes clear that men and women are equal before Allah in terms of accountability due to deeds done by each of them. Surah 16:97 says:

> Whoso doeth that which is right, whether male or female, and has faith, verily to him we will give a new life and life that is good and pure and we will bestow on such their reward according to the best of their actions.

Surah 3:195 says:

> We have believed. Forgive oh Lord, our sins and our mistakes . . . and let us not be shamed on the Day of

Judgment . . .He answered them: Not one good deed will get lost,whoever might have done it, man or women.

Moreover, Surah 24:23 emphasizes in regard to women:

Those who slander and gossip wrongly over respectful and devoted women, shall be condemned in this world and in the world to come and endure immense punishment.

Based on the above verses, the value which Allah accords to men is similar to that which is accorded to women. Both of them bear similar responsibilities before Allah.

Despite the equality between men and women portrayed in the Qur'an above, it remains true that women have not always been permitted to have access to financial resources that the Qur'an makes available to them, prayers and fasting during the menstruating period, and Friday obligatory prayers. In his words, Okon puts it:

In the performance of religious rituals, woman is exempted from prayers and fasting during menstruation and periods of confinement. Woman is exempted from the obligatory prayers on Fridays. Generally, Islam exempts woman from all financial liabilities. Islam extols motherhood as a divine privilege and status of honor and admiration (Surah 31:14–15; 46:15).[9]

Moreover, while the Qur'an shows the equality of men and women in terms of responsibility before Allah, yet it shows great disparity between them in the normal life of society. The Qur'an indicates that men are physically and spiritually stronger than women, and are better and more perfect than women. Surah 2:228 says:

And women shall have rights similar to the rights against them . . . But Men have a degree over them.

Surah 4: 34 says:

9. Okon, "Status of Woman," 22.

Men are the protectors [*qawwamun*] and managers of
the affairs of women, because Allah has given the one
more [strength, *fadilah*] than the other, and because they
support them from their means.[10]

Based on the above verses, women in society, according to the
Qur'an, are not able to control their affairs and situations and need
to be controlled by men. They need to live under the protection of
men in various issues surrounding their lives.

Moreover, women in the Qur'an are depicted as having
critical days in their life cycles where they do not have sound judg-
ments. In those days, a woman needed another woman with sound
judgment to judge for her. Surah 2:282 says:

Get two witnesses out of your own men, and if there are
not two men, than a man and two women, so that if one
of them errs the other can remind her.

In this verse, it is clear that a woman cannot be trustworthy by
the testimony of her alone. A testimony of another woman in a
similar issue is needed in order to make the testimony of that issue
trustworthy.

One of the greatest innovations of the Qur'an over earlier
practices is that women are permitted to inherit and own property. Non-Muslims have generally found great difficulty with the
Qur'anic stipulation that a woman is allowed to inherit property,
but that the inheritance should be only half that of a male. Surah
4:11 says:

Concerning your children, Allah decreed the following:
Male heirs shall have as much as two female heirs.

According to the Islamic understanding, however, the rationale is
precisely that which applies to the verse saying that men are in
charge of women, to take care of them and their families well. As in
the above verse, male children are regarded as the ones to establish

10. For the various definitions of the word *qawwam* by Muslim scholars,
see Orakzai, "Rights of Women," 49–50.

their families, to which they will be responsible, while women will still be under their own husbands after marriages.

Another important aspect facing women in the Qur'an is the dress code and veiling in order to modestly appear in public (*purdah*). Muslim women are supposed to put on the *hijab*, which is said to protect the beauty of the woman from the gaze of men. In Islam, *hijab* is said to be created by God in order safeguard the health of society.[11] Surah 33:59 says:

> Oh Prophet! Tell your wives and daughters, and the believing women, that they should cast their outer garments over their bodies (when abroad): that is most convenient, that they should be known (as such) and not molested.

Moreover Surah 24:31 says:

> Believing women should guard their modesty, should not display their beauty and their ornaments, except what must appear. They should draw their veils over their bosom and not display their beauty, except to their husbands, their fathers . . .

Therefore, the obligation for Muslim women to cover the whole body except the face and hands in order to protect their beauty from the gaze of men is mostly drawn from the above two Qur'anic verses. The problem with Islamic clothing and veiling is that it hardly guards men from unclean thoughts and adulterous desires; such are likely to remain among men despite the veiling of women.

The Qur'an also stipulates the relationship between a man and a woman in marriage affairs. In marriage, the man should have control over his wife in all affairs, including supporting, admonishing her, and her availability in the home.[12] Surah 4:34 says:

> Men are the protectors and managers of the affairs of women, because Allah has given the one more [strength] than the other, and because they support them from their means.

11. Okon, "Status of Woman," 23; cf. Dagher, *Position of Women*, 113–24.

12. Cf. Davids, "Religion, Culture, and the Exclusion," 55.

Surah 4:34 says:

> As to those women on whose part ye fear disloyalty and ill-conduct, admonish them [first], [next] refuse to share their beds, [and last] beat them [lightly]. But if they turn to obedience, seek not against them means [of annoyance]; for Allah is Most High, Great [above you all].

Moreover, Surah 2:223 says:

> Your wives are as a tilth [field] unto you, so approach your tilth when and how you will.

This verse is emphasized in the Hadith thus: "When a man calls his wife to satisfy his desire, let her come to him though she is occupied with the oven" (Mishkat al-Masabih, Hadith 61, duties of husband and wife).

Following the above verses, the support of the husband over his wife includes the payment of dowry as the man is married to his wife. The issue of "beating" in admonishing the wife in Islam has been taken contextually.[13] Others have considered "light beating" as using handkerchiefs, small sticks, etc. Unfortunately, others have not understood the verse at all. This verse is the one which has mostly made the beating of wives legitimate in Islam as a way of admonishing their wives. The issue of availability of the wife for the man's sexual desire is also understood differently. According to the verse above, the burning of the food at the oven is better than the burning of the husband for waiting his wife to satisfy him in his sexual desires.

WOMEN IN THE ISLAMIC TRADITION

The Hadith of Muhammad has even more humiliating statements about women than the Qur'an itself. In the Hadith, women are

13. Beating of wives, though allowed by the Qur'an, is a human violence issue prohibited by law in most countries in the world. In this case, Muslim men beating their wives as a way of admonishing them is discouraged in most countries and by various scholars of Islam (see Okon, "Status of Woman," 25; Dagher, *Position of Women*, 99–107).

charged of having a limited intelligence, of having peculiar biological and physical makeup, regular uncleanness, and the inabil-
ity to exercise their religion fully. Following these charges, women
cannot hold offices as judges, imams, or religious leaders in other
positions.

According to the Hadith, the following is what Mohammad
said when he left the mosque after one of his prayers:

> After Muhammad came out from the place of prayer, he
> saw a few women and told them: "O women give alms,
> as I have seen that the majority of the dwellers of Hellfire
> were you [women]." "Why is this so, Messenger of God?"
> He replied: "You curse frequently and are ungrateful to
> your husbands. I have not seen anyone more deficient
> in intelligence and religion than you." The women asked:
> "What is deficient in our intelligence and religion, Mes-
> senger of God?" He answered: "Is not the evidence of two
> women equal to the witness of one man?" They replied
> in the affirmative. He said: "This is the deficiency in your
> intelligence. Isn't it true that a woman can neither pray
> nor fast during her menses?" The women replied in the
> affirmative. "This is the deficiency in your religion." (Al-
> Bukhari, Hadith 6; Muslim Iman 13; Abu-Dauwd, Sunna
> 15)

Following the view of the Hadith above, women have been considered compassionate people who need to hold positions that need
compassion, such as being medical doctors, nurses, teachers, etc.,
not positions which need judgment.

Mohammad's view of women is similar to that of ancient civilizations of the Greeks. According to Naseef, the Greeks believed
that women were created for only two major purposes: "to procre-
ate and to do the housework."[14] Aristotle, one of the great Greek
philosophers declared thus in regard to women: "Mother Nature
did not endow women with intellectual capacities, therefore their
education should be restricted to housework, mothering, nursing
and other similar tasks."[15] Having declared this, Aristotle placed

14. Naseef, *Women in Islam*, 17.

15. Naseef, *Women in Islam*, 18.

women in the group of people most miserable and unfortunate: "Three categories of people have not the eligibility nor the capacity to make their own decisions: The slave has no volition. The child possesses a will-power but it is incomplete. The woman possesses a will but hers is deficient."[16] Therefore, in a similar way to the ancient Greek civilization, women according to Islamic tradition face oppression and deprevation of their necessary rights. Moreover, they are forced to be under the tyrany of men who in turn absolutely control their lives.

However, ancient Egyptian civilization was different from other ancient civilizations. The Egyptian civilization gave women the necessary civil rights required of them. Naseef writes:

"Women were honoured in Egyptian civilization. The Egyptians entrusted them with their country. They reigned over Egypt, individually or collectively. They drafted the laws, directed foreign affairs and made good politicians. The Egyptians erected statues in memory of their dignity, power and prestige." Although this happy situation did not encompass the whole female population of Egypt, Egyptian civilization remained "the only civilization which entrusted women with a legal status recognised by the nation. It was also the only civilization that granted them full civil rights similar to those given to the male population."[17]

These words indicate that women were not degraded in the Egyptian civilization, as in other ancient civilizations.

ISLAMIC RITES IN WHICH WOMEN PARTICIPATE

Early in the development of the community, women began to find the mosque, the common place of worship, less and less accessible. As separation became the practice more and more, it was not a surprise to find women squeezing out of the more formal aspects of the Islamic faith, forging their own ways of religious response.

16. Naseef, *Women in Islam*, 18.
17. Naseef, *Women in Islam*, 19.

The area of healing and semi-magical practices is one of the areas where substitution took place. The world of spiritual powers needs to be considered in regard to these substitutions because it is where women have been and continue to be primary agents in the relationship between humans and the world of spiritual powers. Women are the ones who know how to deal with the evil *jinn*, to deploy the spirits dwelling in the rivers and fields. They apply special formulas in order to deal with these beings and appropriately display blue beads to challenge the power of the evil eye. In fact, these are just unorthodox practices which continue to make women more isolated from the formal practices or rituals of the Islamic community. Moreover, while these activities provide an arena for women to feel comfortable and in control of men, they still continue to be a powerful group in the lives of many people in the Muslim community, mostly women.

Muslim women engage in prayers. However, prayer for women is usually in the home rather than in the mosque, and does not necessarily happen five times a day. Women also participate in fasting. Female practice does, however, diverge somewhat from that of males, where considerations of purity and space intervene. A woman is not to fast when menstruating, though she is allowed to make up for the days missed. The basic principle is that a woman's person during her menstrual time is not impure, so that she does not transfer impurity to things or persons she touches; though the menstrual blood itself, if spilled, contaminates. The result is that the menstruating woman continues to function fully in society, including in regions where rituals are being carried out.

Another responsibility of all Muslims is almsgiving. Whereas it is the men who determine the amount of good and money to be given in alms, it is the women who take charge of the actual distribution of the same. Muslim women also participate in pilgrimages, but for many, this singular event is but part of the meaning of pilgrimage. Throughout the year they make shorted journeys to the shrines of saints, to their tombs and resting places, to revere and talk with the deceased in the tombs.

Muslim women in various parts of the world participate in rituals referred to as the "*zar* ceremonies." These are rituals designed to rid them of supposed spirit possession. Though men may scoff at these activities, they have to come up with the money needed for their wives to take part in these activities.[18]

PERMITTED ROLES AND IMAGES OF MUSLIM WOMEN

As noted above, the period before the advent of Islam in the Arabian Peninsula is known as *Jahiliyyah*, "the time of ignorance and barbarism." Islam, by contrast, means "submission to the will of Allah." Women played an important role in the establishment of Islam. The prophet's first revelation came to him, according to tradition, in 610 CE when he was forty years old. His wife Khadijah played an important role in his life at this time. She was a woman of dignity and wealth, determined, noble, and intelligent. She proposed marriage to him while he was carrying her goods abroad by caravan. She was the first to believe in God and in his apostle, and in the truth of his message. God assured Muhammad after her death that she had been granted an abode in heaven.

According to the scholar Haifaa Jawad, different from the conventional picture of women in Islam as being cloistered and burked, women in early Islam took part in armed conflicts, either by organizing for and taking care of the wounded, or through playing a crucial part in the actual fighting when it was needed.[19]

SAINTS IN ISLAM

Saints in Islam are both male and female. In order for one to be recognized as a saint, he or she does not need to pass through any process of canonization. One becomes a saint only through some

18. See Mianji, "Zar Spirit Possession," 225; cf. Muhammad, "Sudanese Concept of Beauty."

19. Jawad, "Women and Political Action."

supernatural deeds which that person performs through a dream communication with a living person after that person dies requesting that a place of worship be erected over his or her tomb. Often the woman receives more favors in regard to these dreams, and after the place of worship is erected, she serves as the caretaker of the tomb. This caretaking of the tomb is a position of honor and responsibility. In the general Islamic understanding, saints form a special category of persons who are different from normal earthborn human beings. Their difference is more vivid in the manner that, after death, saints remain very much conscious in their tombs. Saints are reported to continue carrying on activities, such as praying, reciting the Qur'an, and responding to the greetings of their visitors, after their physical death. However, these saints are not worshiped despite their glorification, as this would be very wrong act in the strictly monotheistic Islam.

The most renowned female saint of Islam is, without a doubt, Rabiah al-Adawiyah of early eighteenth-century Basrah in Iraq. Her story, as it has come down to us, touches on several themes of saints' lives: After a humble beginning and sudden conversion, she repented of singing and entertaining and self-denial. Rabiah appears as an early exponent of love-mysticism. She is said to have been beautiful, refused offers of marriage, and had numerous stories in which she was an equally famous female mystic.[20]

While a man may be more likely to ask a saint for strength on the day of judgment and strength to carry out his religious duties, women seek to solve their immediate needs that trouble them in their daily life. In Iraq, some women enjoy hereditary positions of being the *mollas*, i.e., religious teachers. These women receive money for the responsibility of holding public sessions in which stories are read about the life of Hussain the martyred grandson of the Prophet. These are usually activities and occasions for women to meet together away from home under the guise of a traditionally sanctioned activity.

In general, while women in the Islamic world have been segregated, secluded, and historically considered second-class by

---

20. Helms, "Rabiah al Adawiyah"; cf. Sells, *Early Islamic Mysticism*.

males in their communities, they have not been totally without power. They have been able to maintain a degree of control over their own lives and over the lives of men with whom they live through the religious practices described here.

CONCLUSION

Many Muslim women wonder that the fruits of liberation in the West are too many broken marriages, women left without the security of men who would provide for them, deteriorating relations between men and women and sexual license that appears as rank immorality. In contrast, they see the Islamic systems affirmed by the Qur'an as one in which male authority over them ensures their care and protection.

To many women, Islam provides a structure in which the family is solid, children are inculcated with lasting values, and the balance between the responsibility between man and woman is one in which absolute equality is prized through cooperation and complementarity.

CHAPTER REVIEW

1. How were women conceived during the *Jahiliyyah* period, i.e., in the period of ignorance?

2. What does the Qur'an say about what was going on in the Arabian Peninsula during the period of ignorance?

3. Has the emergence of Islam reformed the women-subjugating traditions of the pagan Arabian Peninsula? In what way?

4. What does the Qur'an, the scriptures of Islam, say about the role of women in issues of marriage, divorce, inheritance, ownership of properties, dress code, and seclusion?

5. How is the woman depicted in the Islamic tradition (*hadith*)?

6. What is the role of women in terms of sainthood in Islam?

Chapter 7

WOMEN WITHIN BUDDHISM

INTRODUCTION

IN THE BEGINNING OF her article entitled "Buddhism," Barnes states: "Gotama the Buddha lived 2500 years ago and the religion he founded has since spread far beyond the boundaries of its original homeland in Nepal and Northern India."[1] According to Barnes, canonical literature of Buddhism was produced in India and this forms the normative Buddhist literary tradition. She points out that those women in early Indian Buddhism were exposed to egalitarianism. This meant that the same teachings were given by Buddha to female and male disciples, and the very same spiritual path was mapped out for them, opened to all.[2]

The Buddhist movement began as an ascetic but also as a rebellious movement of members of the social elite. Its founder, Siddhartha Gotama, was born into a noble family that ruled over the area that is now on the Indian-Nepalese border. At the age of twenty-nine, he left his home to pursue the life of an ascetic wanderer in search of enlightenment. He had a yearning for a

---

1. Barnes, "Buddhism," 105.
2. Barnes, "Buddhist Women," 105.

state of mind beyond suffering and death. When close to death by starvation, he made one more attempt at that coveted spiritual breakthrough. When meditating under a fig tree, he gained insight into the law of karma, i.e., that activities in one's past life determine one's present situation, and that this life is but one in an endless chain of embodiment. It became clear to him that only through moral and mental discipline and ruthless inquiry into the true nature of things would one gain Nirvana.[3]

The sacred texts of Buddhism number in the tens of thousands and are preserved in numerous classical languages of Asia. Since the end of the nineteenth century, non-Asian people in Europe, Africa and North America have adopted Buddhism, making it one of the fastest growing religions. However, in absolute numbers, Buddhism is still a minority religion.[4]

In Buddhism, as Barnes writes, it is believed that a person "desires because one is extremely fond of oneself. A person normally believes that she or he is unique and that somewhere within is a special essence, a soul or self which is precious, and different from every other individual in the world and which is well worth providing for in every way."[5] This notion is thought to be a mistake. As such, to eradicate this false belief in the self and in the permanence of things, Buddhists are to follow the path of meditation and moral discipline, which leads them to powerful, liberating insight into the true nature of existence, by which one's mind is opened and changed.[6]

An order of monks for both women and men was formed. The order for women was called *bhiksuni-samgha*, and that of the men was called *bhiksu-samgha*. These orders were formed so as to foster a life fully devoted to the pursuit of *Nirvana*.[7] Note that *Samgha* is an order, a community, association, or company of monks or nuns.

3. Neumaier, "Women in Buddhist Traditions," 81.
4. Neumaier, "Women in Buddhist Traditions," 80.
5. Barnes, "Buddhism," 106.
6. Barnes, "Buddhist Women," 106.
7. Barnes, "Buddhist Women," 106.

WOMEN IN BUDDHIST MONASTICISM

Barnes states thus in regard to the formation of the male and female orders of monks after the Buddha's enlightenment: "Soon after the Buddha's own enlightenment he formed an order of monks, male renunciants of ordinary worldly life, and a few years after that he was asked by his foster mother and aunt . . . to establish a similar order for women. But he refused her request three times, and only upon the intervention of Ananda, his kinsman and constant attendant, did he agree to let an order be founded."[8] However, his condition was that the women in the founded order should agree to adhere to the eight rules which would equate them to what is followed by monks, but being subordinate to them.[9]

The Buddha accepted the capability of women to become *arhants*, that is, people who have achieved Nirvana. However, there was a gradual evolvement of the whole accumulation of regulations for both monks and nuns, despite the existence of special rules which applied only to nuns. An example of this is the eight chief rules. These eight rules require that the superiority of the monk be recognized by each nun, and each nun should treat every monk as her superior and senior regardless of the age of the monk. The rules forbid a nun to ever revile or admonish any monk. In addition, they direct that all sisters' formal ceremonies should be carried out under the guidance or in the presence of the monks' *samgha*. Moreover, there are penances for erring nuns.[10] However, the vast majority of the hundreds of monastic rules are the same for monks and nuns, such as living a life of renunciation, having their heads shaved, and wearing (in most cases) similar robes. There were other rules for the nuns alone as follows:

1. Every nun, regardless of her seniority was junior to even the youngest monk.

8. Barnes, "Buddhism," 107.
9. Barnes, "Buddhist Women," 107; Barnes, "Buddhism," 107.
10. Barnes, "Buddhist Women," 107.

2. Nuns cannot spend the rainy season in a place where no monk is available (in order to instruct them in the monastic discipline).

3. Nuns ought to ask the monks for setting the day of the confession ceremony and providing exhortations to them.

4. After the rainy season, the nun has to inquire before the monks' and nuns' samgha whether any fault can be laid to her charges.

5. A nun found guilty of serious offence has to undergo discipline before both samghas.

6. A woman who has completed the two year novitiate must ask the monks' samgha for full initiation.

7. A nun must never revile or abuse a monk.

8. Nuns cannot reprimand monks for violation of monastic rules and proper conduct, but monks can reprimand nuns.[11]

Whether these rules were actually established by Buddha or were later added by monks acrimonious of women's presence in the *samgha*, the nuns were effectively relegated to a subordinate position within the *samgha* and had little hope of ever assuming leadership roles there.

Indeed, both nuns and monks had renounced ordinary life in the world and had gone on to follow the way of the Buddha. In terms of spiritual exercises, nuns and monks do the same things, follow the same routines, live the same sort of disciplined lives, and practice the same form of meditation techniques. They even look alike, for they shave their heads and wear the same robes. In every way, nuns and monks seem to appear as the very same. However, by imposing rules on nuns which would place them in a permanently inferior position in all their interactions with monks, the monks were reserving for themselves the control and leadership of the entire *samgha*.[12] Barnes states thus: "Undoubtedly

11. Neumaier, "Women in Buddhist Traditions," 77–80.

12. Barnes, "Buddhist Women," 108.

such a desire to exercise authority over nuns rather than to accept complete assimilation with them came from traditional ideas about the proper relative positions of men and women prevailing in India at the time."[13] The monks controlled the *samgha* and were apparently the majority, and the public eye was on them more than were the nuns.

THE BUDDHIST LAY WOMEN

Nuns were not the only women in the early Buddhist communities. There were laywomen as well who received a greater acceptance and respect from the monks than the nuns themselves. These laywomen were devoted to the *dharma* (true Buddhist teaching) and had great support from the *samgha* through their generous giving. This willingness to give was very important to the well-being of the *samgha* in terms of its economy. The role of the laity was to attend to the well-being of the *samgha* and remain spiritual followers of the clergy. Hence, the monks taught them the *dharma* as a return to their gifts.[14]

The teachings offered did not make any distinction whether some kind of them belonged to laywomen as opposed to those teachings which belonged to laymen. The distinction was visible when someone on occasion asked a question specifically relating to women. According to Barnes, the real issue for the status of women in Buddhism is not that Buddhist monks roundly despised women; rather, the issue is that they sought to keep women out of all positions of authority, in theory and practice. Barnes adds that Buddhist literature shows relatively little interest in theories of women's character, largely because monks in early times were not thinking of controlling female fertility, and at the same time, there was no supreme male deity to be concerned about. However,

13. Barnes, "Buddhism," 108.

14. Barnes, "Buddhist Women," 109; cf. LeVine, "Dharma Education," 138.

she adds that what has always been important in Buddhism, as in other religions, is who keeps authority in their hands.[15]

The Buddhist laywoman stands in the shadow of the renouncing male, the monk providing him with food and alms when he comes at her door. She is praised for her piety, devotion for the faith, generosity, patience, and her role of mother and wife. In pre-Buddhist India, a woman's life was measured according to how useful she was to her father, brother, husband, or son. A woman independent from a male relative or husband had no place in society, as she was an abnormality. However, within the early Buddhist communities, a woman gained acceptance and status on her own right. This improved status of women within Buddhist communities becomes clear regarding inheritance practices. Certain women became the sole owners of property.[16]

Buddhist laywomen are hardly visible within the hierarchy. These women have, with very few exceptions, little public visibility or influence. However, the laywoman remains a person who quietly affirms the main concepts of Buddhism, which are compassion, humility, patience, and generosity. In so doing, she supports the monks with food donations and creates within her family a vibrant atmosphere in which to practice Buddhist teachings.[17]

CONCLUSION

We have seen in this chapter that Buddhism did not remain moribund in India; rather, it was transmitted by missionaries beyond the Indian boundaries by the third century BCE. This transmission and propagation of Buddhism was done by the endorsement of the emperor Asoka. By the beginning of the Common Era, Buddhism had been transported across central Asia and into China. In China, there were some orders of nuns established in the fourth century CE. Unlike the orders of nuns in other Buddhist countries,

15. Barnes, "Buddhist Women," 114.
16. Neumaier, "Women in Buddhist Traditions," 92.
17. Neumaier, "Women in Buddhist Traditions," 93.

the ones in China have survived as an unbroken tradition until the present.

The Buddhist women in China find the nuns order a very important institution since it affords women an opportunity to live a respectable, active life outside the traditional family structure.[18] As such this has provided an alternative lifestyle for women in China and wherever else the movement was strong. The opposition that faced women in the *samgha* was that of taking positions of authority. In all Buddhist sects the world over, men have always dominated and still dominate. As Tsomo, quoting Diana Paul, writes: "Like Judaism and Christianity, Buddhism is an overwhelmingly male-created institution dominated by a patriarchal power structure. As a consequence of this male dominance, the feminine is frequently associated with the secular, powerless, profane, and imperfect."[19]

However, it should be acknowledged that the study of women in Buddhism is a relatively new field to date. It is only in recent times that modern scholars have begun to examine seriously the manifold questions relating to the place of women in Buddhism as a religion. Tracing to its original teachings, Buddhism did not offer any doctrinal resistance in regard to the acceptance of women and men as being equally capable of spiritual attainment of Nirvana. In fact, the mainstream Buddhism held this thought throughout the centuries. However, it wasn't until women started to question their status that there emerged a theological controversy surrounding some efforts to prove women as inferior to men in terms of *Karma*, and therefore as being incapable of the attainment of the ultimate state of being, Buddhahood. Hence this claim is supported by Buddhist texts "that assert women's guilt by association with procreation and refer to women as fickle, sexually voracious, contentious, and evil."[20]

18. Barnes, "Buddhist Women," 123.

19. Tsomo, "Is the Bhiksuni Vinaya Sexist?," 45.

20. Tsomo, "Is the Bhiksuni Vinaya Sexist?," 45.

CHAPTER REVIEW

1. Who was the founder of Buddhism, when did it start, and how?

2. What is the meaning of *bhiksuni-samgha* and *bhiksu-samgha*?

3. Are women capable of achieving Nirvana according to Buddhism?

4. Briefly discuss the role of women according to Buddhist teachings.

Chapter 8

WOMEN WITHIN HINDUISM

INTRODUCTION

AT THIS BEGINNING OF the chapter, we should quote the words of Aruna Gnanadason, the then-executive secretary of the All India Council of Christian Women, a subunit of the National Council of Churches in India, who also worked as the secretary of the World Council of Churches, Women's Desk. Gnanadason writes about the existence of feminist theology in India in the 1990s:

> Feminist theology is still not recognized as widely as it should be in India. Clouded in controversy and viewed with suspicion, it has in fact no tradition at all in India. If anything, the Bible has been used to legitimize the low status of women. The main arguments against the women's movement and against feminism are often derived from the Bible. Whenever women have protested at the discrimination faced by them in Church and society, the Bible has been used to indicate that the secondary status of women is divinely ordained—woman was made after man, she brought sin and death into the world, Christ had no women disciples, Paul called on women to be silent in church and to be obedient to their husbands— these are some of the more commonly used arguments

to support such a stand. Women are urged, therefore, to be submissive wives and live according to the biblical "teachings" on womanhood, if they are to be happy.[1]

Gnanadason further adds, "Though there is some movement towards change of these attitudes, the low status accorded to women and the imprisonment of women's voice have their roots in a distorted understanding of the Scriptures."[2] This was the situation in India for women Christians.

The questions which arise from the above statement are the following: What was the situation of women in the native Hindu religion? How do the Hindu scriptures and Hindu tradition view women's status within the Hindu religion? Hinduism is a complex religion; and unlike many Western religions, it is also a way of life. The origin of materials for studying Hindu traditions in this chapter came from two sources: the first is the traditional Hindu literature, and the second is the enlightenment models. Though classical Hindu texts give the impression of being immutable, Hindu practices have and remain fluid and flexible, allowing for adaptations. There are concepts, rituals, and even gods and goddesses that have evolved and faded away. In sum, Hindus have, over the centuries, been able to keep their culture vibrant, interpret sacred texts, and adapt practices from the ancient Indus valley civilization. In this sense, as Gnanadason puts it, "Christianity in India has tended, in fact, to be much more patriarchal than the surrounding culture in India because of its institutional, theological, and doctrinal rigidity."[3]

In order to place women at the center stage in studying the Hindu tradition, there has been a development of scholarship that begins with women's experiences and focuses on women, thereby placing them at the center and not the margins. According to Narayanan, this approach involves asking new questions and reconceptualizing categories that have been used conventionally.[4] This

1. Gnanadason, "Feminist Theology," 59.
2. Gnanadason, "Feminist Theology," 59.
3. Gnanadason, "Feminist Theology," 59.
4. Narayanan, "Hinduism," 56–57.

is one way that could aid in correcting the invisibility of women created by traditional male scholarship. Given that, there are many areas in Hindu tradition where a woman can look for encouragement. Narayanan singles out three. The first is the philosophical sphere, which will avail to us that the soul is without gender. Thus, unlimitedly, in the quest for liberation, gender is irrelevant. In some Hindu literature, souls (whether they belong to male or female bodies) may be gendered female, thereby leveling the field in the potential for liberation.[5]

The second area is the sphere of social institutions, more precisely the field of dharma. These are actions that would be sanctioned by appeal to *atmatushti*, or the happiness of one's soul, an appeal to one's conscience. This gives institutional room for women to live their religious lives to the fullest potential.

The third and last area to which a woman can look for hope and encouragement is the historical factor: Here, after patient researching, one will find women who made a mark in traditionally male spheres, giving a long list of poets, patrons, and philosophers.[6]

In Hinduism, women, especially from royal families, were patrons, liberal benefactors of temples and other institutions. They gave land and even donated money. Revenues derived from these were then used for major festivals. Women also gave large number of jewels to the temple. One example of such a woman was Samavai. It is known that Samavai endowed money to celebrate some festivals and consecrate a processional image of the Lord, a silver replica of the main deity. Within a short time she donated large parcels of land to be sold and the proceeds be used for major festivals.[7] These donations depict the generosity of women to the service of the faithful.

Women who are wives have more roles and activities to be done daily involving more than just caring for the household; they also involve religious ceremonies. Despite the fact that Verdic rituals are entrusted to Brahmin men, Hindu women still have

5. Narayanan, "Hinduism," 56–57.
6. Narayanan, "Hinduism," 56–57.
7. Narayanan, "Hinduism," 49.

important places in religious services. For example, the wives of Brahmin priests can both keep the home and assist their husbands on activities relating to rituals performed.[8]

The queens of the *Chola* dynasty are said to have been patrons of temples and religious shrines of the *shiva* community of South India around the tenth century. Others, like the South Indian queen Sembiyan Mahadevi gave major donations to many Shiva temples. Such occasions cause us to underscore women's religious roles. They also show us that different women had independence of lifestyle and finances.

A careful look at Hindu history shows many women poets who wrote prose treatises, and participated in discussions or even debated on philosophy. An example is Tarigonda Venkamamba, who lived from 1800–1866.[9] There were also many women philosophers. These challenged other male philosophers with questions in public debates. These women were both philosophers and composers. They were able to continue in poetry and philosophy and avail a number of compositions. In the philosophical sphere, according to many Hindu texts, the soul is without gender and so, ultimately, gender is irrelevant.

Tirukkoneri Dasyai lived in the thirteenth and fourteenth centuries. She wrote a commentary combining both Sanskrit and Tamil, and in it she quotes the Vedas and other Sanskrit texts profusely. This implies that she had extensive access to at least to those parts of the Vedas that had salvific and theological import. It is proper to indicate that Dasyai had access to this vast learning and was able to express herself creatively. In other words she was a learned and articulate woman from one of the prominent Hindu traditions.[10]

---

8. Narayanan, "Hinduism," 56–57.

9. Narayanan, "Hinduism," 54.

10. Narayanan, "Hinduism," 54–55.

WOMEN AND THE HOME IN HINDUISM

Hinduism places women as the main supporters in the life of the home. They are responsible for making the home live through sustaining the family and keeping the deities happy. Sadarangani clearly describes the functions of women in the home when she writes:

> In India, women maintain the home and, more importantly, the kitchen. They are the caregivers of the children and they establish consistently and well-being of their entire family. In the Hindu home, however, there are the deities to take care of as well. Women have the responsibility of ensuring that the needs of these deities are met. They feed them, bath them, and cloth them regularly in order to make them happy.[11]

Hence, since most people, especially in the urban setting, have no time to visit temples as done in villages, the activities of women at the home towards deities makes the home an important place in Hinduism to make the religion live among people's lives.

As their domain, women in Hindu tradition enjoy cooking and feeding the family with not only delicious, but also nutritious, food. For the Hindu women, Sadarangani states, "cooking is not only the way to please their families, but [also] a way of producing something they themselves enjoy."[12] Sadarangani quotes some women as saying: "If I let my husband cook, not only would he make a mess in the kitchen, but I would not be eating the food I found tasty."[13] In this case, "Taking pride and pleasure from one's own work is very important to these women as well as things in the kitchen being done in a structured and ordered manner which the men were not expected to maintain."[14] Hindu women enjoy seeing that they have played their part in producing food which other people and deities in the home enjoy eating, keeping the order of

11. Sadarangani, "Modernized Hinduism," 3.
12. Sadarangani, "Modernized Hinduism," 9.
13. Sadarangani, "Modernized Hinduism," 9.
14. Sadarangani, "Modernized Hinduism," 9.

the kitchen as is required, and recognize that they hold the secrets of producing exceptional foods which their husbands are not able to maintain. For them, cooking does not become a burden, but a duty and a pleasure at the same time.[15]

MEN AND WOMEN IN THE HINDU TRADITION

What can we say about the above-stated relationship between men and women in the Hindu home? What can be said is that the Hindu tradition portrays some sort of patriarchal kind of relationship between men and women. One of the typical characteristics of a patriarchal tradition, as discussed in chapter two above, is locating women in the home and its duties. Basharat states thus regarding the way Hinduism considers women: "Hinduism, as a religion opposes the fundamental rights of the female clan. The *Vedas*, Scripture of Hindus is quite hostile to its women no matter what. According to it, women happen to be inhuman and are subject to no primary civil liberties. The society, thus, ignored all kinds of rights owned by the women and thus, in ancient era all led a hopeless life."[16]

Basharat further notes that the lives of women in Hinduism are governed by the Laws of Manu. In these laws, women are considered subordinate to men. Barashat, quoting from the famous book called *Laws of Manu*, writes: "In childhood a female must be subject to her father, in youth to her husband, when her lord is dead to her sons: a woman must never be independent . . . Though destitute of virtue, or seeking pleasure [elsewhere], or devoid of good qualities, [yet] a husband must be constantly worshiped as a god by a faithful wife."[17] The Laws of Manu further emphasize:

> Day and night, women must be kept in dependency by the males of their [families], and if they attach themselves to sensual enjoyments, they must be kept under

15. Sadarangani, "Modernized Hinduism," 10.

16. Basharat, "Contemporary Hindu Women," 243.

17. Basharat, "Contemporary Hindu Women," 243.

one's control . . . Through their passion for men, through their mutable temper, through their natural heartlessness, they become disloyal towards their husbands, however carefully they are guarded in this world. Knowing their disposition, which the Lord of creatures laid in them at the creation, to be such, [every] man should most strenuously exert him to guard them.[18]

Hence, according to the Hindu scriptures (the Vedas) the Hindu women were predetermined to being under the control of men in a similar way that men can control various other objects.[19]

However, the situation is changing in the twenty-first century. Hindu women are struggling to regain their civil rights in society. Quoting Gabrielle, Basharat writes: "At present, we find the Indians struggling to achieve the much deserved social liberty and status as done by the Negro community, back in the 1960s."[20] Taking ideas from Sarasvati, Basharat adds that the education which Indian women were denied following the traditions of the past is now offered to them. Currently, there are highly educated women in India despite the existence of some fundamentalists who try to stick to the past traditions of denying education to Hindu women.[21]

In the twenty-first century, India has witnessed many women rising into higher ranks of leadership, as compared to the past times "when women were considered epidemic rather than human."[22] Women in India are militant fighters for rights focusing on issues of "gender, class, caste, economic status, and the like,"[23] which are characteristic of the hierarchical stratification of the Indian society at large. Chako describes the Indian caste system as being "a pyramid of earthenware pots set one on top of the other. Not only are Brahmins and Kshatriyas at the top and Shudras and untouchables at the bottom, but within each earthenware pot, men are at the top

---

18. Basharat, "Contemporary Hindu Women," 243.

19. Basharat, "Contemporary Hindu Women," 243.

20. Basharat, "Contemporary Hindu Women," 244.

21. Basharat, "Contemporary Hindu Women," 244.

22. Basharat, "Contemporary Hindu Women," 245.

23. Basharat, "Contemporary Hindu Women," 245.

and women of that caste are at the bottom like crushed and wasted powder."[24] Moreover, the goddess cult said to be practiced in India portrays that women were not an oppressed entity but ones with power in society. Sadarangani writes: "'worship of the Goddess's life-giving aspects has survived, though primarily in women's worship,' which shows the importance of the Goddess tradition to women as they have a religious figure who they can relate with."[25] In addition, Hedman taking ideas from Hellman affirms that "there seems to be an unspoken idea that worshiping goddesses is a source of power and inspiration for women."[26] Hence, through the relationship with the deities in the home, the Hindu women conform to the meaning of religion according to Hinduism. According to Sadarangani, "Religion, especially Hinduism, is a method of nurturing and caring for the deities in hopes that they will care for you back, and throughout history women have commonly been viewed caregivers. This relationship puts women at the center of the religious practices."[27]

HINDU WOMEN AND THE MANDIR

What do women do as their daily routine towards the deities apart from feeding them? Sadarangani says that their major responsibility is to clean the deities, the *mandir*,[28] and putting them in order within the *mandir*. In length, Sadarangani says:

> after bathing in the morning, clean the entire [*mandir*], taking out each and every Divinity and wiping it down with a clean cloth (usually these cloths are kept aside specifically for cleaning the deities and are not used for any

24. Chako, "One and the Many," 48.

25. Sadarangani, "Modernized Hinduism," 13.

26. Hedman, "Hindu Goddesses," 2.

27. Sadarangani, "Modernized Hinduism," 13.

28. A *mandir* is the home of the deities. It is "a structure that is in the form of a house, temple, or box where the images of the deities are kept" (Sadarangani, "Modernized Hinduism," 14n6).

other purposes). They then wipe down the inside of the *mandir* and end the cleaning process by carefully placing each deity back in their specific spot, which is, of course memorized.[29]

In so doing, the Hindu women are considered as caring people, not only for the Hindu families, but also the deities and their houses.

CONCLUSION

Devotion is exalted in the *Vedas* and many other texts because many hold that it is knowledge that leads one to liberation. In matters of liberation, it matters least whether one is a woman or a man, since all are eligible for it. The paths of devotion, knowledge and selflessness are open to every human being. It is this ultimate knowledge that Hindu women have sought, to lead them to immortality.

Though classical Hindu texts may give the impression of being immutable, Hindu practices have been fluid and flexible, allowing for adaptations and adjustments. Basharat reiterates:

> despite the fact of *Vedas*, the holy scripture of Hindus (being quite anti-feminism and thus instituting in males superiority), females of Hindu community have travelled a long way. From the old conventions of sati, *pardah*, illiteracy and being an asset of the males, the women have made a huge come back. They have not only earned social and economic development but also the political liberty. In this age, many women have renounced their orthodox views about their religion and thus joined the more modern mainstream.[30]

This statement means that there is room for assimilation and redefinition of situations in the Hindu society which can allow for Hindu women to forge ahead in their daily religious devotions.

---

29. Sadarangani, "Modernized Hinduism," 14.

30. Basharat, "Contemporary Hindu Women," 247.

CHAPTER REVIEW

1. What is the role of women in the home according to the teaching of Hinduism?

2. What is the status of women according to the Laws of Manu?

3. Briefly describe the role of Hindu women to the *mandir*.

4. What is the status of women according to the Vedas, the Hindu scriptures?

Chapter 9

ECOFEMINISM AND THE SACRED[1]

INTRODUCTION

ECOLOGICAL CRISIS IS WELL-DOCUMENTED the world over. According to Radford Ruether, this crisis includes some aspects such as toxic air pollution, soil erosion, and destruction of rain forests which are vivid in various parts of the world. Since human population increases in the world, the stated aspects remain a threat to planetary life and their effects expand rapidly.[2] In her words, Ruether says:

> There is toxic pollution of air, water and soil, soil erosion and desertification, the thinning of ozone layer, allowing cancerous radiation, exhaustion of supplies of fossil fuels, destruction of rain forests, causing climate changes as well as accelerated extinction of species. All these phenomena are expressions of the threat to the basis of planetary life wrought by the rapid expansion of technological methods of production, transportation, heating

1. This title is borrowed from Carol J. Adam's *Ecofeminism and the Sacred*, published in 1993.

2. See Ruether, *New Woman, New Earth*; Ruether, "Ecofeminism and Healing Ourselves."

and waste disposal, the effects of which are multiplied by rapidly expanding human population.[3]

According to her, the changes in nature due to the above stated activities prompt a close examination of the growing population, industrial development, changes in modern technology, and waste disposal strategies which enhance environmental degradation. The changes of nature also prompt a revisit of the "deeper cultural and spiritual problems underlying patterns of social and ecological domination, rooted in the splitting of mind and body, the alienation of the human concept of the self from the physical world."[4] Therefore, the emergence of ecofeminism, as a movement within feminism, has a link with the question of nature and its destruction by the above-stated aspects on the one hand, and the status of women on the other.

What then is ecofeminism, and what is its historical background? The concept of ecofeminism is a combination of the radical ecology movement and feminist movement. It was coined by Frenchwoman Francoise d'Eaubonne in 1974 in her book *Le Feminisme ou la Mort* (*Feminism or Death*).[5] "For d'Eaubonne the term was meant to describe how the human race could be saved by women initiating an ecological revolution, as a way to counter the oppression of women that is one and the same as the oppression and destruction of nature."[6] To some scholars, ecofeminism belongs to the third wave of feminism, but to others it belongs to deep ecology. However, it belongs to none of the two but brings together feminism and deep ecology, critiquing the dominant philosophical attitudes towards nature. Ecology examines how natural communities function to sustain a healthy web of life and how they become disrupted causing the death of animal and plant life. Ecology emerged as a combination of socioeconomic and biological study in the late sixties to examine just how human use of nature is

3. Ruether, "Ecofeminism and Healing Ourselves," 51.

4. Ruether, "Ecofeminism and Healing Ourselves," 51.

5. Salman, "Ecofeminist Movements," 853; cf. Tollefsen, "Ecofeminism, Religion and Nature," 90–91.

6. Tollefsen, "Ecofeminism, Religion and Nature," 90–91.

causing pollution of soil, air, water, and destruction of the natural system of plants and animals, threatening the base of life on which humans depend. In that case, ecofeminism looks "at cultural and social concerns dealing with the relationship that the oppression of women has with the degradation of nature."[7] As Tollefsen clearly states, "The idea that women are, because of their womanhood, spiritually close to nature is central to ecofeminist thought, and is manifested in many forms of [nature] religion—both in the west and the east—often in the form of worshiping the inner goddess that resides in women."[8] Therefore, ecology stands at the heart of ecofeminism linking human systems and systems of nature.

Adams writes: "Ecofeminism identifies the twin dominations of women and the rest of nature. To the issues of sexism, racism, classism, and heterosexism that concern feminists, ecofeminists add naturalism—the oppression of the rest of nature. Ecofeminism argues that the connections between the oppression of women and the rest of nature must be recognized to understand adequately both oppressions."[9] Since the "Oppression of women and the environment have been 'twin subordinations,'"[10] as Salman and Tollefsen say, deep ecology goes a step further in examining the symbolic, psychological, and ethical patterns of the destructive relations that humans have had with nature and how to replace such relations with a life-affirming culture. In the words of Cuomo, "ecofeminism stresses the depth to which human realities are embedded in ecological realities, and the fact that we are all composed of physical and conceptual connections and relationships."[11] However, according to Sallie McFague, the link between justice and ecological issues arose in the light of a dualistic, hierarchical mode of Western thought in which a superior and an inferior are correlated: male/female, white people / people of color, heterosexual/homosexual, culture/nature, human/nonhuman, etc. These

7. Salman, "Ecofeminist Movements," 853.

8. Tollefsen, "Ecofeminism, Religion and Nature," 91.

9. Adams, "Introduction," 1.

10. Salman, "Ecofeminist Movements," 853.

11. Cuomo, "On Ecofeminist Philosophy," 1.

are often normatively ranked, one superior to another, which is then deemed inferior.

As such, there is the ancient and deep identification of women and nature, an identification that profoundly touches upon the very marrow of our being, i.e., our birth from the bodies of our mothers and our nourishment from the body of the earth. Salman points out that

> Women world wide[*sic*], are often the first ones to notice environmental degradation. Women are the first ones to notice when the water they cook with and bathe the children in, smells peculiar: they are the first to know when the supply of water starts to dry up. Women are the first to know when the children come home with stories of mysterious barrels dumped in the creek: they are the first to know when children develop mysterious ailments.[12]

To McFague, the power of nature and that of women to give birth to life inescapably creates a connection between the two. In sum, the status of women and the status of nature are generally considered commensurate.[13]

An in-depth exploration of the connection between domination of women and domination of culture has been made on two levels: the cultural-symbolic level and the socioeconomic level. These levels are elaborated below:

CULTURAL-SYMBOLIC LEVEL

At this level, Rosemary Ruether asserts that traditionally, males were engaged in work that was more occasional and more prestigious. In situating themselves in this, they had the privileges of leisure. The male power that grew led them to define the culture for the whole society, socializing males and females to these view points. The result was male monopoly of culture. The earth in this case is then systematically linked to women, i.e., plant in it and

---

12. Salman, "Ecofeminist Movements," 183.

13. McFague, *Body of God*, 85.

let life arise. Ruether shows these by using examples from the Hebrew, Greek, Christian, and the reformation traditions.[14] As such, patriarchal culture has identified women as being closer to nature and belonging to the nature side of the culture-nature dichotomy. Salman reiterates this point thus: "Women are seen in sync with nature, working in union with it, while men have a hierarchical relationship with nature in which their actions try to dominate it. This view poses the idea that men's control over nature has created an ecological crisis in much of the world today."[15]

THE SOCIOECONOMIC LEVEL

Here the focus is on how women as a gender group, their bodies, and their work have been colonized by patriarchy as a legal, economic, social, and political system, and how colonization of women's bodies and work function as the invisible substructure for the exploitation of nature. Here we consider the way that women have been assigned to works such as gardening, caretakers of small children, weavers, cooks, cleaners, etc., as indicated. Meanwhile a number of men denigrate these works and link them to the identification of women with the subhuman status. In general, since women are linked to environment and its care, and while there is a hierarchical relationship between men and nature (domination of nature), there are socioeconomic underpinnings of women's domination and that of nature.

But how can we transform cultural symbolic patterns of our religious culture that uphold the system of domination? From the perspective of healing, it is wise to consider possibilities such as

1. Worship of the feminine nature. Here ecofeminists see a transformation of culture towards worship of a feminine nature as key to restoring such paradisal nature and society,

2. Drawing upon interconnections between women and nature. The stereotypes should explode in each other. There is in

14. Ruether, "Eco-feminism and Healing," 35–49.

15. Salman, "Ecofeminist Movements," 853.

Western culture two images of woman as nature in complementary tension. Woman as evil nature and woman as boun-
tiful, ever nurturing, nature as paradise,

3. Deconstruction of dualisms. Here the dualism to be decon-
   structed is that of women as nature and men as culture, one
   that deconstructs all sides of this false division,

4. Need for both cultural and structural changes through poets,
   artists, theologians, etc.

Following the above points, theologians have suggested various
ways to reconceptualize the meaning and significance of Christ so
as to capture insights that will be useful for our interconnected
world. According to Maseno, "Several approaches have been offered to help explore the intersection between Christology and
ecology. Kwok Pui-Lan suggests three possibilities: first, the organic model for Christ, where organic images are consistently used
in order to underscore the interrelatedness of the human and the
natural realms."[16] Here the emphasis is on models that elaborate on
Jesus as the true vine and the believers being the branches. These
images bring to sharp focus the direct association of Christology
and ecological matters.

Second, "Jesus as an epiphany, which identifies the Christic
presence in and among humans."[17] Jesus is said to be living among
and in believers in different passages of the Bible. This life of Jesus
in humans is Christ's presence, which is felt in and among those
who live and serve God. Humans, as the family of God, call upon
and believe in Jesus' presence in and among them; in so doing, the
presence of Jesus comes and is felt in the many congregations and
church gatherings the world over.

Third, "Jesus as the Wisdom of God, which draws upon the
concept of Jesus as Sophia-God."[18] Therefore, as pointed out above,
Jesus as Sophia is said to be living among and in believers in different passages of the Bible. The indwelling of Jesus among and in

16. Maseno, "Towards an African Inculturated Sophiology," 125.

17. Maseno, "Towards an African Inculturated Sophiology," 126.

18. Maseno, "Towards an African Inculturated Sophiology," 125.

his people involves the use of African categories to reinterpret and rearticulate Jesus' name in African terms and life conditions.

We are of the opinion, as Maseno puts it, "that an African Sophiology could be gleaned from wisdom traditions, which attest to the sacredness in nature, within the various African cultures through inculturation; such a Sophiology gives a contextual interpretation which takes African people's thought forms and worldviews seriously. This approach is helpful for conceptualizing the significance of Christ in our contemporary world."[19]

Following the above assertion, Kwok Pui-Lan, opines that the implication of Jesus as Sophia for people is greatly noticeable in various cultures around the world. For Pui-Lan, Jesus as Sophia has found home in the wisdom traditions of a variety of cultural contexts. It is relevant cross-culturally to most people who struggle to get a suitable language to speak about Christ. It is within this interpretative sphere that it is possible to consider Jesus as Sophia and draw a link between Sophia and the ancient wisdom traditions in Africa. As just noted, some African myths provide insights into the sense of the sacred in nature. Consequently, one can provide an interpretation of Jesus as Sophia in Africa through African myths by exploring these myths in order to creatively develop an African inculturated sophiology that emphasizes ecological concerns.[20] In so doing, the meaning of Jesus as Sophia is made possible in the context of African culture and its historical periods.

CONCLUSION

In full view of the present perilous times and ecological deterioration, human beings have to see themselves as earthlings, not as aliens or tourists on the planet. Such a focus would mean that there is a concentration on God subjectively existing in the processes of the macrocosm, including the planet. Such a focus would mean that the divine concern includes all of creation and

19. Maseno, "Towards an African Inculturated Sophiology," 127.
20. Maseno, "Towards an African Inculturated Sophiology," 127.

that there would be a cosmocentric focus rather than an anthropocentric focus.

We could look out for clues in various cultures—for example, in Hinduism, Buddhism, and Taoism, where there is a vision of letting go of overwhelming egotistic individualism and the harmonization of the dynamic forces at work in the cosmos and in the society. Many indigenous people in Africa, Latin America, etc., have gained new respect from they way they created their own bioregional culture that sustained the human community as a part of the community of animals, plants, earth, sky, ancestors, and descendants.

The central question that remains unanswered is probably about the vitality of ecofeminism as a movement. Has it fulfilled its goal? The goal of the ecofeminist movement is clearly stated by Warren as quoted in Cuomo: "Minimally, the goal of ecofeminist environmental ethics is to develop theories and practices concerning humans and the natural environment that are not male-biased and that provide a guide to action in the prefeminist present."[21] Based on this goal, is ecofeminism practically and philosophically vital? Some scholars have noted that though it is philosophically elegant, it is less vibrant in actions, which makes it lose power and remain marginal in the world of emancipatory movements. In Salman's article, for example, she concludes that, "Sadly, it is the gap between philosophy and action which keeps Ecofeminism tenuous and peripheral as a movement."[22]

CHAPTER REVIEW

1. What is meant by the term "ecofeminism"?

2. Discuss the two levels that enable us to explore in-depth the connection between domination of women and domination of culture, i.e., the cultural and the socialeconomic levels, according to Rosemary Ruether.

21 Cuomo, "On Ecofeminist Philosophy," 6.
22 Salman, "Ecofeminist Movements," 862.

3. What does it mean to depict Jesus as Sophia? How can we draw a link between Jesus as Sophia and the ancient traditions in Africa?

BIBLIOGRAPHY

Ackermann, Denise, and Tahira Joyner. "Earth-Healing in South Africa: Challenges to Church and Mosque." In *Women Healing Earth: Third World Women on Ecology, Feminism, and Religion*, edited by Rosemary Radford Ruether, 121–34. New York: Orbis, 1996.

Adams, Carol J. "Introduction." In *Ecofeminism and the Sacred*, edited by Carol J. Adams, 1–12. New York: Continuum, 1993.

Adams, Carol J., and Marie M. Fortune, eds. *Violence Against Women and Children: A Christian Theological Sourcebook*. New York: Continuum, 1995.

Adelman, Penina Villenchik. *Miriam's Well: Rituals for Jewish Women Around the Year*. Fresh Meadows, NY: Biblio, 1986.

Adler, Margot. *Heretic's Heart: A Journey through Spirit and Revolution*. Boston: Beacon, 1997.

Aldredge-Clanton, Jann. *In Search of the Christ-Sophia: An Inclusive Christology for Liberating Christians*. New London, CT: Twenty-Third Publications, 1994.

———. *In Whose Image? God and Gender*. New York: Crossroad, 1990.

Amoah, Elizabeth. "Theology from the Perspective of African Women." In *Women's Visions: Theological Reflection, Celebration, Action*, edited by Ofelia Ortega, 1–7. Geneva: WCC, 1995.

Anderson, Leona M., and Pamela Dickey Young. *Women and Religious Traditions*. Don Mills, Ontario: Oxford University Press, 2004.

Barnes, Nancy J. "Buddhism." In *Women in World Religions*, edited by Arvind Sharma, 105–34. Albany: State University of New York Press, 1987.

———. "Buddhist Women and the Nuns' Order in Asia." In *Engaged Buddhism: Buddhist Liberation Movements in Asia*, edited by Christopher S. Queen and Sallie B. King. Albany: State University of New York Press, 1996.

Basharat, Tahira. "The Contemprary Hindu Women of India: An Overview." *A Research Journal of South Asian Studies* 24.2 (2009) 242–49.

Beavis, Mary Ann. "Who is Mary Magdalene?" https://www.baylor.edu/content/services/document.php/199647.pdf.

Bediako, Kwame. *Theology and Identity: The Impact of Culture upon Christian Thought in the Second Century and in Modern Africa*. Oxford: Regnum, 1992.

Bevans, Stephen B. *Models of Contextual Theology*, Maryknoll: Orbis, 2005.

Booley, Ashraf. "Divorce and the Law of *Khul*: A Type of No Fault Divorce Found within an Islamic Legal Framework." *Law, Democracy & Development* 18 (2014) 37–57.

Casimir, Ani, *et al.* "The Church and Gender Equality in Africa: Questioning Culture and the Theological Paradigm on Women Oppression." *Open Journal of Philosophy* 4 (2014) 166–73.

Chako, Mani. "The One and the Many: Emerging Christology in an Indian Context." In *Discovering Jesus in Our Place: Contextual Theologies in a Globalized World*, 45–65. Kashmere Gate, Delhi: Indian Society for Promoting Christian Knowledge, 2003.

Chikwelu, Emmanuel J. "Never Marry a Woman with Big Feet: The Proverbial Oppression of Women in Igbo African Culture: An Investigation of the Semantics of Female Devaluation in Igbo African Proverbs." Master's thesis, University of Kwa-Zulu Natal, 2017.

Chisale, Sinenhlanhla Sithulisiwe. "Patriarchy and Resistence: A Feminist Symbolic was Interactionist Perspective of Highly Educated Married Black Women." Master's thesis, University of South Africa, 2017.

Clarke, Adam. *The New Testament of Our Lord and Saviour Jesus Christ: The Text Carefully Printed from the Most Correct Copies of the Present Authorized Version including Marginal Readings and Parallel Texts with a Commentary and Critical Notes Designed as a Help to a Better Understanding of the Sacred Writings*. Volume 1. New York: Emory and Waugh, 1831.

Clifford, Anne M. *Introducing Feminist Theology*. Maryknoll: Orbis, 2001.

Cudworth, Erika. *Developing Ecofeminist Theory: The Complexity of Difference*. New York: Palgrave Macmillan, 2005.

Cuomo, Chris. "On Ecofeminist Philosophy." *Ethics and the Environment* 7.2 (2002) 1–11.

Dagher, Hamdun. *The Position of Women in Islam*. Villach, Austria: Light of Life, 1995.

Davaney, Sheila Greeve. "Continuing the Story, but Departing the Text: A Historicist Interpretation of Feminist Norms in Theology." In *Horizons in Feminist Theology: Identity, Tradition, and Norms*, edited by Rebecca S. Chopp and Sheila Greeve Davaney, 198–214. Minneapolis: Fortress, 1997.

Davids, Nuraan. "Religion, Culture, and the Exclusion of Muslim Women: On Finding the Reimagined Form of Inclusive-Belonging." *Knowledge Cultures* 4.4 (2016) 46–59.

Denton, Lynn Teskey. *Female Ascetics in Hinduism*. Albany: State University of New York Press, 2004.

Dube, Musa. "'Go Therefore and Make Disciples of all Nations' (Matt. 28:19a): A Postcolonial Perspective on Biblical Criticism and Pedagogy." In

BIBLIOGRAPHY

Teaching the Bible: The Discourses and Politics of Biblical Pedagogy, edited by Fernando F. Segovia and Ann Tolbert, 224–46. Maryknoll: Orbis, 1998.

———. *Postcolonial Feminist Interpretation of the Bible*. St. Louis: Chalice, 2000.

Epstein, Richard A. "Liberty, Patriarchy and Feminism." *University of Chicago Legal Forum* 89 (1999) 89–114.

Eriksson, Anne-Louise. *The Meaning of Gender in Theology: Problems and Possibilities*. Uppsala: Eriksson, 1995.

Ferree, Myra Marks, *et al.*, eds. *Revisioning Gender*. Thousand Oaks: Sage, 1999.

Frostin, Per. *Luther's Two Kingdoms Doctrine: A Critical Study*. Lund: Lund University Press, 1994.

Gnanadason, Aruna. "Feminist Theology: An Indian Perspective." In *Readings in Indian Christian Theology*, edited by R. S. Sugirtharajah and Cecil Hargreave, 59–72. London: SPCK, 1993.

Haddad, Beverly. *African Women's Theologies of Survival: Intersecting Faith, Feminisms, and Development*. PhD diss., University of Natal, Pietermaritzburg, 2000.

Harmer, Elizabeth C. "'One Woman with Many Faces': Imaginings of Mary Magdalene in Medieval and Contemporary Texts." Master's thesis, McMaster University, Hamilton, Ontario, August 2005.

Hedman, Hanna. "Hindu Goddesses as Role Models for Women? A Qualitative Study of Some Middle Class Women's Views on Being a Woman in the Hindu Society." Master's thesis, University of Gävle, Sweden, 2007.

Helms, Barbara Lois. "Rabiah al Adawiyah as Mystic, Muslim and Woman." Master's thesis, McGill University, 1993.

Herzel, Susannah. *A Voice for Women: The Women's Department of the World Council of Churches*. Geneva: World Council of Churches, 1981.

Hinga, Theresa. "Between Colonialism and Inculturation: Feminist Theologies in Africa." *Feminist Theology in Different Contexts*, edited by Elisabeth Schussler-Fiorenza and Mary Shawn Copeland, 26–34. London: SCM, 1996.

———. "Jesus Christ and the Liberation of Women in Africa." In *The Will to Arise: Women, Tradition, and the Church in Africa*, edited by Mercy Amba Oduyoye and Musimbi R. A. Kanyoro, 183–95. Maryknoll: Orbis, 1992.

Humm, Maggie. *Dictionary of Feminist Theory*. 2nd ed. Columbus: Ohio State University Press, 1989.

Hussein, Jeylan W. "The Social and Ethno-Cultural Construction Masculinity and Femininity in African Proverbs." *African Study Monographs* 26.2 (2005) 59–87.

Ifechelobi, J. N. "Feminism: Silence and Voicelessness as Tools of Patriarchy in Chimamanda Adichie's *Purple Hibiscus*." *African Research Review* 8:4 (2014) 17–27.

Jackson, Stevi, and Jackie Jones, eds. *Contemporary Feminist Theories*. Edinburgh: Edinburgh University Press, 1998.

Jawad, Haifaa A. "Women and Political Action." In *The Rights of Women in Islam: An Authentic Approach*, 83–96. New York: St. Martin's, 1998.

Jóhannsdóttir, Nína Katrín. "Patriarchy and the Subordination of Women: From a Radical Feminist Point of View." Master's thesis, University of Iceland, 2009.

Jones, Serene. *Feminist Theory and Christian Theology*. Minneapolis: Fortress, 2000.

Kandiyoti, Deniz. "Bargaining with Patriarchy." *Gender and Society* 2.3 (1988) 274–90.

Kanyoro, Musimbi. "Engendered Communal Theology: African Women's Contribution to Theology in the 21st Century." In *Talitha Cum! Theologies of African Women*, edited by Nyambura J. Njoroge and Musa W. Dube, 158–80. Pietermaritzburg: Cluster, 2001.

Kasomo, Daniel. "The Role of Women in the Church in Africa." *International Journal of Sociology and Anthropology* 2.6 (2010) 126–39.

Katrak, Ketu H. "Teaching Aidoo: Theorising via Creative Writing." In *Essays in Honour of Ama Ata Aidoo at 70: A Reader in African Cultural Studies*, edited by Anne V. Adams, 140–45. Oxfordshire: Ayebia, 2012.

King, Ursula, ed. *Feminist Theology from the Third World: A Reader*. London: SPCK, 1994.

Kostenberger, Andreas J., and David W. Jones. *God, Marriage, and Family: Rebuilding the Biblical Foundation*. Wheaton: Crossway, 2010.

Lerner, Gerda. *The Feminist Thought of Sarah Grimke*. New York: Oxford University Press, 1998.

LeVine, Sarah. "Dharma Education for Women in the Theravada Buddhist Community of Nepal." In *Buddhist Women and Social Justice: Ideas, Challenges and Achievements*, edited by Karma Lekshe Tsomo, 137–54. Albany: State University of New York Press, 2004.

Lewis, Ruth Bartlett. "Angeline Grimké Weld, Reformer." PhD diss., Ohio State University, 1962.

Lochhead, Joyce A. "'Turning the World Upside Down': Women Abolitionists and the Women's Rights Movement." Master's thesis, Northwest Missouri State University Maryville, Missouri, November, 2014.

Maluleke, Tinyiko. "An African Theology Perspective on Patriarchy." In *The Evil of Patriarchy in Church, Society and Politics*, 31–36. A consultation held at Mount Fleur Conference Centre, Stellenbosch on 05 and 06 March, 2009.

Maponda, Anastasie M. "The Impact of the Circle of Concerned African Women Theologians: French Zone on Church and African Theology Issues." *Verbum et Ecclesia* 37.2 (2016) a1597. http://dx.doi. org/10.4102/ ve.v37i2.1597.

Maseno, Loreen. "Towards an African Inculturated Sophiology: The Case of African Wisdom Traditions from Myths for Ecological Concerns." In *Religion and Ecology in the Public Sphere*, edited by Celia Deane-Drummond and Heinrich Bedford-Strohm, 125–38. London: T. & T. Clark, 2011.

Maseno, Loreen, and B. Moses Owojaiye. "African Women and Revival: The Case of the East African Revival." *European Journal of Research in Social Sciences* 3.3 (2015) 28–36.

Maseno, Loreen, and Daniel Kasomo. "A Critical Appraisal of African Feminist Theology." *International Journal of Current Research* 2.1 (2011) 154–62.

Maseno, Loreen, and Susan M. Kilonzo. "Engendering Development: Demystifying Patriarchy and its Effects on Women in Rural Kenya." *International Journal of Sociology and Anthropology* 3.2 (2011) 45–55.

Maseno-Ouma, Loreen. "Patriarchy Ridiculed and Turned Upside Down: The Role and Place of Humour in Esther 1:1–22." In *The Bible and Sociological Contours: Some African Perspectives: Festschrift for Professor Halvor Moxnes*, edited by Zorodzai Dube et al., 89–96. New York: Lung, 2018.

Maseno-Ouma, Loreen Iminza. *Gendering the Inculturation Debate in Africa.* Berlin: Lambert, 2011.

Mbiti, John. "The Role of Women in African Traditional Religion." *Blojlu's Blog*, n.d. https://blojlu.wordpress.com/news-makers/the-role-of-women-in-african-traditional-religion/.

McFague, Sallie. *The Body of God: An Ecological Theology.* Minneapolis: Fortress, 1993.

Mianji, Semnani. "Zār Spirit Possession in Iran and African Countries: Group Distress, Culture-Bound Syndrome or Cultural Concept of Distress?" *Iran Journal of Psychiatry* 10.4 (2015) 225–32.

Mmadike, Benjamin Ifeanyi. "The Igbo Perception of Womanhood: Evidence from Sexist Proverbs." *Research on Humanities and Social Sciences* 4.18 (2014) 98–104.

Muhammad, Baqie Badawi. "The Sudanese Concept of Beauty, Spirit Possession, and Power." *Folklore Forum* 26.1/2 (1993) 43–67.

Naseef, Fatima Umar. *Women in Islam: A Discourse in Rights and Obligations.* International Islamic Committee for Women & Child 1. Cairo: International Islamic Committee for Woman & Child, 1999.

Nasimiyu, Wasike. "Christology and an African Woman's Experience." In *Faces of Jesus in Africa*, edited by Robert Shreiter, 70–81. 9th ed. New York: Orbis, 2005.

Nayaranan, Vitsudha. "Hinduism." In *Her Voice, Her Faith: Women Speak on World Religions*, edited by Katherine Young and Arvind Sharma, 11–58. Cambridge Massachusetts: Westview, 2003.

Neumaier, Eva K. "Women in Buddhist Traditions." In *Women and Religious Traditions*, edited by Leona M. Anderson and Pamela D. Young, 80–107. Ontario: Oxford University Press, 2004.

Neale, Diana. "Out of the Uterus of the Father: A Study in Patriarchy and the Symbolization of Christian Theology." *Feminist Theology* 5.8 (1996) 8–30.

Nfah-Abbenyi, Juliana Makuchi. *Gender in African Women's Writing: Identity, Sexuality and Difference.* Bloomington: Indiana University Press, 1997.

BIBLIOGRAPHY

Nunes, C., and H. J. M. Van Deventer. "Feminist Interpretation in the Context of Reformational Theology: A Consideration." *Die Skriflig* 43.4 (2009) 737–60.

Obododimma, Oha. "The Semantics of Female Devaluation in Igbo Proverbs." *African Study Monographs* 19.2 (1998) 87–102.

Oduyoye, Mercy Amba. *Daughters of Anowa: African Women and Patriarchy.* Maryknoll: Orbis, 1995.

———. "Feminist Theology in an African Perspective." In *Paths of African Theology,* edited by Rosino Gibellini, 168–81. London: SCM, 1994.

———. *Introducing African Women's Theology.* Sheffield: Sheffield, 2001.

———. "Reflections from a Third World Woman's Experience and Liberation Theologies." In *The Eruption of the Third World: Challenge to Theology: Papers from the Fifth International Conference of the Ecumenical Association of Third World Theologians, August 17–29, 1981, New Delhi, India,* edited by Virginia Fabella and Sergio Torres, 246–55. Maryknoll: Orbis, 1983.

———. *Who Will Roll the Stone Away? The Ecumenical Decade of the Churches in Solidarity with Women.* Geneva: WCC, 1990.

Oduyoye, Mercy Amba, and Musimbi R. A. Kanyoro, eds. *The Will to Arise: Women, Tradition, and the Church in Africa.* Maryknoll: Orbis, 1992.

Okon, Etim E. "The Status of Woman in Islam." *IOSR Journal Of Humanities And Social Science* 10.2 (2013) 21–27.

Olajubu, Oyeronke. "A Socio-cultural Analysis of Yoruba Women and the Re-Imaging Christianity." *Feminist Theology* 16.3 (2008) 312–23.

Orakzai, Saira Bano. "The Rights of Women in Islam: The Question of 'Private' and 'Public' Spheres for Women's Rights and Empowerments in Muslim Societies." *Journal of Human Rights in the Commonwealth* 2.1 (2014) 42–51.

Papanek, Hanna. "Purdah: Separate Worlds and Symbolic Shelter." *Comparative Studies in Society and History* 15.3 (1973) 289–325.

Parratt, John. *Reinventing Christianity: African Theology Today.* Grand Rapids: Eerdmans, 1995.

Pechilis, Karen, ed. *The Graceful Guru: Hindu Female Gurus in India and the United States.* New York: Oxford University Press, 2004.

Pemberton, Carrie. *Circle Thinking: African Women Theologians in Dialogue with the West.* Leiden: Brill, 2003.

Phiri, Isabel Apawo. "HIV/AIDS: An African Theological Response in Mission." *The Ecumentical Review* 56.4 (2004) 422–31.

Pillay, Miranda N. "The Anglican Church and Feminism: Challenging 'the Patriarchy of Our Faith.'" *Journal of Gender and Religion in Africa* 19.2 (2013) 53–71.

Pinkham, Mildreth Worth. *Women in the Sacred Scriptures of Hinduism.* New York: AMS Press, 1967.

Pui-Lan, Kwok. "Engendering Christ." In *Toward a New Heaven and a New Earth: Essays in Honor of Elisabeth Schüssler Fiorenza,* edited by Fernando Segovia, 300–313. Maryknoll: Orbis, 2003.

Ruether, Rosemary Radford. "Ecofeminism and Healing Ourselves, Healing the Earth." *Feminist Theology* 3 (1995) 51–62.

————. "Ecofeminism: Symbolic and Social Connections of the Oppression of Women and the Domination of Nature." *Feminist Theology* 3 (1995) 35–51.

————. *Mary: The Feminine Face of the Church.* London: SCM, 1979.

————. *New Woman, New Earth: Sexist Ideologies and Human Liberation.* Boston: Beacon, 1975.

Russel, David. "Introduction to the Publication of Papers." In *The Evil of Patriarchy in Church, Society and Politics,* 2–3. A consultation held at Mount Fleur Conference Centre, Stellenbosch on 05 and 06 March, 2009.

Sadarangani, Monique M. "Modernized Hinduism: Domestic Religious Life and Women." Master's thesis, University of Hawaii, 2005.

Salman, Aneel. "Ecofeminist Movements—From the North to the South." *The Pakistan Development Review* 46.4 (2007) 853–64.

Schussler-Fiorenza, Elisabeth. *Rhetoric and Ethics: The Politics of Biblical Studies.* Minneapolis: Fortress, 1999.

Sells, Michael Anthony. *Early Islamic Mysticism: Sufi, Qur'an, Miraj, Poetic and Theological Writings.* New York: Paulist, 1996.

Selokela, Oniccah N. "African Women Overcoming Patriarchy: A Study of Women in Apostolic Faith Mission (AFM) Church in Rustenburg–South Africa." Master's thesis, University of KwaZulu-Natal, South Africa, 2005.

Sharma, Arvind, and Katherine K. Young, eds. *Her Voice, Her Faith: Women Speak on World Religions.* Cambridge: Westview, 2003.

Sibanda, Nhlanhla. "An Analysis of the Significance of Myths and Proverbs as African Philosophies of Peace and Justice: A Case of the Ndebele, Shona and Tonga Tribes from Zimbabwe and the Igbo from Nigeria." *IOSR Journal Of Humanities And Social Science* 20.4 (2015) 1–6.

Smith, Jane I. "Islam." In *Women in World Religions,* edited by Arvind Sharma, 235–50. Albany: State University of New York Press, 1987.

Stanton, Elizabeth Cady. *The Woman's Bible.* Boston: Northeastern University Press, 1993.

Sulaimani, Faryal Abbas Abdullah. "The Changing Position of Women in Arabia under Islam during the Early Seventh Century." Master's thesis, University of Salford, 1986.

Sultana, Abeda. "Patriarchy and Women's Subordination: A Theoretical Analysis." *The Arts Faculty Journal* (July 2010–June 2011) 1–18.

Tamez, Elsa. "Latin American Feminist Hermeneutics: A Retrospective." In *Women's Visions: Theological Reflection, Celebration, Action,* edited by Ofelia Ortega, 77–89. Geneva: WCC, 1995.

Tappa, Louise. "The Christ Event from the Viewpoint of African Women: Protestant Perspective." In *With Passion and Compassion, Third World Women Doing Theology,* edited by Virginia Fabella and Mercy Amba Oduyoye, 30–35. Maryknoll: Orbis, 1988.

Taysense. "The Role of Women in Africa (Great African Proverbs)." http://www.ligali.org/forums/index.php?showtopic=553.

Togarasei, Lovemore. "The Legacy of Circle Women's Engagement with the Bible: Reflections from an African Male Biblical Scholar." *Verbum et Ecclesia* 37.2 (2016) a1582. http://dx.doi.org/10.4102/ve.v37i2.1582.

Tollefsen, Inger B. "Ecofeminism, Religion and Nature in an Indian and Global Perspective." *Alternative Spirituality and Religion Review* 2.1 (2011) 89–95.

Tong, Rosemarie, and Tina Fernandes Botts. *Feminist Thought: A More Comprehensive Introduction.* New York: Routledge, 2018.

Trible, Phyllis. "Eve and Adam: Genesis 2–3 Reread." http://academic.udayton.edu/michaelbarnes/E-Rel103/RG4-Trible.htm.

Tsomo, Karma Lekshe. "Is the Bhiksuni Vinaya Sexist?" In *Buddhist Women and Social Justice: Ideas, Challenges and Achievements,* edited by Karma Lekshe Tsomo, 45–72. Albany: State University of New York Press, 2004.

Wadley, Susan S. "Women and Hindu Tradition." *Signs* 3.1 (1977) 113–25.

Walby, Sylvia. *Theorizing Patriarchy.* Cambridge: Basil Blackwell, 1990.

Wood, Johanna Martina. "Patriarchy, Feminism and Mary Daly: A Systematic-Theological Inquiry into Daly's Engagement with Gender Issues in Christian Theology." PhD diss., University of South Africa, 2013.

Young, Pamela Dickey. *Feminist Theology/Christian Theology: In Search of Method.* Minneapolis: Augsburg Fortress, 1990.